BLACK MAYORS
AND SCHOOL POLITICS

GARLAND REFERENCE LIBRARY OF SOCIAL SCIENCE
VOLUME 1048

Black Mayors and School Politics
The Failure of Reform in Detroit, Gary, and Newark

Wilbur C. Rich

Garland Publishing, Inc.
New York and London
1996

Library of Congress Cataloging-in-Publication Data

Rich, Wilbur C.
    Black mayors and school politics : the failure of reform in Detroit,
Gary, and Newark / Wilbur C. Rich.
        p.   cm. — (Garland reference library of social science ; vol.
1048)
    Includes index.
    ISBN 0-8153-2066-3 (hc : alk. paper). — ISBN 0-8153-2340-9
(pbk. : alk. paper)
    1. Politics and education—Michigan—Detroit.   2. Politics and educa-
tion—Indiana—Gary.   3. Politics and education—New Jersey—Newark.
4. Afro-American mayors—Michigan—Detroit.   5. Afro-American mayors—Indiana—Gary.   6. Afro-American mayors—New Jersey—Newark.
7. Detroit (Mich.)—Politics and government.   8. Gary (Ind.)—Politics and
government.   9. Newark (N.J.)—Politics and government.   I. Title.
II. Series: Garland reference library of social science ; v. 1048.
LC90.M5R53   1996
379.73—dc20   95-51042
                                                                                    CIP

Printed on acid-free, 250-year-life paper
Manufactured in the United States of America

To all the Rich women
who have taught in public schools

Lydia L. Wiggins Rich, my mother
Patricia Ann Rich Bell, my sister
Carolyn Rich Walker, my sister
Jean R. Miller Rich, my wife
Brenda Owen Rich, my sister-in-law.

Contents

Figures and Tables

Figures

Tables

Preface

Some people believe that if inner-city black children had excellent schools, they would perform better in them. Well, maybe. Granted, schools are a part of the problem, but they are not all of the solution. Schools are only buildings where teachers, administrators, and students interact. Learning is a more much complex process. There are many forces arrayed against an inner city child that preclude him/her from mastering the education process. Among these forces are poverty, family instability, disruptive classroom environments, and incompetent teachers. There seems to be no end to research and speculation about how to overcome these forces. Compensatory education strategies such as Head Start, tracking, and privatization have not worked. The gap between black and white children continues to widen. Accordingly, we must face the fact that the repair of public schools, in general and inner city schools in particular, requires an unprecedented massive overhaul. Obviously, we should start at the local level, but the overall reform task is literally beyond the capacity of local government. No group realized this more than the black politicians who began taking over city politics at the end of the 1960s.

When I started this book I was searching for some evidence that black politicians were changing the status quo. What I found were highly politicized school systems continuing the status quo but in deep denial. Black politicians have succumbed to the mighty forces of what I call the public school cartel (PSC). After weathering several protracted battles for control of schools, the politicians surrendered to the PSC. This book will explain why and how black politicians lost the school reform fight.

The project began as a study of the relationship of black mayors to schools. I asked the question: Do black mayors make a difference for schools? If not, why? The study examines the period after the 1954 *Brown* decision and the outset of black challenges for the mayoralty in the late 1960s. I also include brief histories of the school system to highlight the roles African Americans played before the takeover of the city politics. It must be noted that school districts are separate special purpose governments charted by the state. Although mayors do not have formal control over schools, including those who appoint board members, their informal control can be significant. Despite their fiscal and political autonomy, no school district can safely ignore the mayor of their city.

Originally, this was designed as a two year project, but it became clear that more time was needed to fully understand this political situation. I chose three school systems for this study: Detroit, Michigan; Gary, Indiana; and Newark, New Jersey. The book presents a systematic survey of school politics in these three cities, giving particular emphasis to local reform efforts. This book differs from other books on the subject in its sustained consideration of the political calculations of the actors and the symbols they have used to promote their interest.

Research on the book began in 1989. It took five years to come up with a manuscript that could be read by colleagues. I must confess a new admiration for those who have kept the faith that American schools can be reformed. I have gone from being a true believer to an atheist. So this book will come out in the middle of a troubled Clinton Administration when the national attention has shifted to another agenda. The children in Detroit, Newark, and Gary who entered school the year this book was started are old enough to know how the lack of a political and pedagogic solution to their learning needs may handicap them for the rest of their lives.

Numerous individuals helped me understand school politics and black politics. Among the Detroiters were Coleman Young, Clara Rutherford, Bennett Nowicki, Alonzo Bates, Dr. Arthur Jefferson, John Elliot, Thomas Stallworth, and Dr. Ed Simpkin. Garyites included Richard Hatcher, Clarence Currie, Steve Morris, Patrica Dilts, Christine Swan Clay, James Dowdell, Dr. Ernest Jones, Heron Battle, Sandra Irons, Dr. Della Burt, Darlene Maloney. Among the interviewees in Newark were Kenneth Gibson,

Columbus Salley, Rebecca Doggett, Robert Braun, Wynona Lipman, Donald K. Tucker, and Daniel Gibson, Jr.

Several people read all or part of the manuscript in one draft or another, and I owe a debt to them for keeping me on the right road. Their comments and suggestions were extremely helpful. They are: Sam Gove, Martin Kilson, Brendan O'Flaherty, Hanes Walton, Rachel Rich, Carla Sapford, and Janet Anderson. I would also express my appreciation to the National Conference of Black Political Scientists and the Conference of Minority Public Administrators for allowing me to read drafts of chapters as panel papers. I discovered Jeffrey Mirel's *The Rise and Fall of an Urban School System* after the manuscript had been completed, but it was very useful for the revisions of the Detroit chapter. Although our interpretations of events differ, his work helped me understand Detroit school politics.

The project was sponsored by the Spencer Foundation, Wayne State University, and Wellesley College. The views expressed in this book are those of the author and should not be ascribed to the funding sources whose assistance is acknowledged above.

Black Mayors
and School Politics

CHAPTER 1

Introduction:
The Search for Firm Ground

During the 1970s and 1980s a new governing elite took over several urban school systems. A coalition of black school board members, central administration staffs, and teacher union leaders assumed control over the policymaking apparatus of inner city public schools. This takeover was noteworthy because black Americans were major players in the new governing coalition. In the sixties blacks demanded a place at the decision-making table. In some cities they now have the whole table. There are black mayors, school board members, superintendents, black central office staff members, principals and teachers. Yet school performance among inner city schools has not shown any discernible or sustained improvement. Inner city schools still exhibit what Jonathan Kozol called "savage inequalities."[1] These schools are operating just above the level of those in Third World countries. It is an American tragedy that seeks relief. The new governing coalitions presented themselves as harbingers of fundamental change in the way schools are governed and the way children learn. What has followed the new school administrations has been an apocalyptic governing style that fails all involved, both leaders and the public. These groups may survive this tragedy, but the real damage is to the children of these wretched schools. Promises were made to the children that haven't been kept.

Data collected in the early 1990s reveal a seemingly insurmountable gap continuing between white and black children. In 1992 test scores found black nine-year-olds were 33 scale points behind their white cohorts in reading, 27 points behind in math, 39 points in science. In 1993 the SAT scores for blacks were 91 points below those of whites in the verbal section and 106 points lower in the math section. Granted this was an improvement over the 119 and 139 respective point gaps in 1976.[2] These data are not good news for blacks entering an increasingly competitive and knowledge-intensive job market. The gap may be closing but not fast enough. The nation has good reasons to be unhappy about these scores.

In many inner city communities, a smoldering resentment exists against the quality of education available in these schools, resentment which could erupt into a firestorm of anti-public school protest. Education leaders are desperately trying to gain control over the situation but to no avail. School politicians often behave like keystone cops, chasing the culprits while falling all over themselves in the process. Increasingly, regular city politicians, who are not a part of the official school governing coalition, see themselves as possible saviors of the public schools. Their offer of rescue has not been met with enthusiasm. To understand this reluctance, one must acknowledge the myth that the public schools supposedly operate in a parallel policy universe insulated from partisan politics. History reveals, however, that the schools have never been free of local politics. Conversely, school officials have been forced to become good politicians to protect their institutions from the grinding gears of municipal politics.

Given this history and the susceptibility of school officials to partisan politics, this book examines the relationship between black politicians and school policy. Second, it delves into the school's role in an uncertain local economy. Third, it analyzes the failure of school reform under black leadership. In many ways the book is a response to this environment. The thrust of the book is that educational policy-making is political, and the participants are incredibly skillful at staying in power. This skill, however, does not always make them good trustees for the schools.

Why do local partisan politicians want to encroach publicly on school governing coalition turf? Schools are one of the major linchpins of the urban economy. The factor affects "white flight," middle-class black flight, and the ability of the city to attract businesses. In addition, the increased interest in school policy is a result of the emergence of school districts as major employers in cities. School districts have big budgets, hiring thousands of local residents and purchasing a variety of products and services. City politicians covet these financial assets of the district. The district is empowered to raise local taxes, sell bonds, and make long-term contracts. School districts generate millions of dollars for the local economy. This cornucopia of economic opportunity cannot escape the ubiquitous patronage arm of local politicians. Indeed, this arm has been found reaching deep into the money-lined pockets of local districts. It is not uncommon for a mayor or city council to become very involved in millage elections, which are referendums to continue or increase property taxes for schools. Mayors have played major roles in the selection of school superintendents and in decisions regarding the location of new schools.

The spending power of the board of education is so important to the local economy that public-school officials are lobbied incessantly. Douglas Yates has called this "street-fighting pluralism" in which various interest groups fight over a shrinking pie.[3] Inner city school decisions are more intense because of limited economic opportunities in American Rust-Belt cities. The school pie feeds many families, and slicing it is a major event within the local economy.

This economic significance of school politics has produced a cartel-like governing entity. It is not a cartel in the pure economic sense, but its behavior is cartel like. A coalition of professional school administrators, school activists, and union leaders maintains control of school policy to promote the interest of its members. Membership in the cartel confers income, status, and perks. Members agree to follow cartel norms and rules. Violation of those can result in sanctions by the cartel.

Obviously, power within the cartel's governing groups is not evenly distributed. Most urban school superintendents are recruited from outside the community and have little local political power but have more status nationally. Nathan Grundstein calls such administrators "nationals" and are essentially interchangeable between cities.[4] The board of education is the legal governing body in the cartel and is usually the center of power for the members. The school district's permanent central administrative staff also wields considerable influence over policy since it is charged with the implementation of decisions. The relationship of staff to other members of the cartel is a matter of mutual role taking as board, staff, and union reflect each other on policy. They get to know each other so well that they can anticipate each other. The central staff are also the holders of institutional memory. As a result they have considerable power in the cartel. School or community activists are considered the "locals." Community activists are recruited to show community involvement and support for cartel activities. Once recruited , they are socialized into norms of the cartel. Community activists are also mobilized to work in school board elections and to serve on the elected board. The political networks of the community activists are used to explain board policy. Although union leaders represent the teachers, they also play a more critical role in the school board election process. Control over the board election process has yielded the union leaders considerable influence over cartel policy.

Once entrenched, a school cartel usually remains in power regardless of opposition to its policies. Despite the turnover in cartel membership, a socialization process of new members precludes a radical departure from the norms of the cartel. Public dissatisfaction with policy is generally viewed by cartel members as a threat to its organizational integrity and commitment. They treat such dissatisfactions as products of bad press, misunderstanding, and political grandstanding by potential candidates for the board. No one could possibly be more committed to quality education for children than their elected officials and teachers. Accordingly, the cartel members believe that they are just as reform-minded as any outside school reform group. The disagreement with outside groups is over the definition of school reform and the feasibility of proposed changes.

School reform refers to the effort to achieve equity and excellence in the classroom through changes in school practice, personnel, or structures. Reform has a procedural and substantive dimension. Procedural reform involves the introduction of new and different pedagogical processes. Substantive reform involves changes in governance, institutional structures and personnel. David Tyack makes a distinction between fundamental and incremental school reform. Since schools are by nature conservative institutions, Tyack believes that they will be more amenable to incremental than fundamental change.[5] Accordingly, procedural reforms are considered incremental and are gradually adopted into the school routine. Substantive reforms are usually resisted because they are difficult to implement but also because they disrupt organizational routine.

This explains why school reform candidates and their proposals are viewed with suspicion. Between elections the cartel regards complaints about policy as the work of dissidents and muckraking reporters. Opposition groups are often handled by discrediting their spokespersons, coopting their proposals, or sacrificing the superintendent.

There is no assumption of permanent tenure for a superintendent. Termination is routine if, in the judgment of the cartel, change, or the appearance of change, is needed. The test of the institutionalization of a particular reform measure is whether it survives the tenure of the superintendent who introduced it or was associated with it. Superintendents and their reforms are usually jettisoned together. It is not uncommon for a system to spend thousands of dollars on a new reform program only to see it abandoned with the hiring of a new superintendent. Although superintendents are not always the source of reform, they are usually hired with the promise that they will change things. The public expects inner city superintendents to deal with a catalog of school deficiencies. This "fix it" mandate may protect the superintendent for the first two or three years. Later, the superintendent is more exposed to the whims of the cartel.

The cartel's expectations of a superintendent are different from those of the public. They evaluate the superintendent according to their internal needs. If their unity is jeopardized, then the superintendent is expendable. Since superintendents cannot protect the cartel's interest, there is no reason to guarantee a long tenure. Indeed, the longer the superintendent is in office, the less power he or she has in school policy. The first sign of trouble is usually when the central staff leaks reports to the press that they are dissatisfied with the superintendent. It is not uncommon for a union leader to have a public dispute with a superintendent. Once the process of removal begins, it is almost impossible for a superintendent to stop it. For the cartel the best superintendent is one that accepts the blame for what has gone wrong and leaves quietly.

Although school cartels resemble elements of urban regimes[6] and exhibit responses highlighted in Lutz and Wang's Dissatisfaction Theory,[7] cartel politics are very different. Stone's regimes, coalitions of businessmen and elected politicians, maximize economic development.[8] School cartels, on the other hand, are primarily interested in self-perpetuation. Unlike regimes, they cannot change the quality of service by edict. They have control over the decision-making process but cannot regulate the impact of those decisions on student performance. Simply put, their policy decisions cannot improve the quality of school performance or, for that matter, change fundamentally the impact of a school's environment on its students.

This is not to suggest that there are no disagreements within the cartel or that the public is powerless in its relationship with this group. As this book will show, the history of school systems indicates that there have been several periods of social disequilibrium between the governing structure and the public. During prolonged periods of disequilibrium, official policies are questioned and challenged. Dissatisfaction, a cumulative process, can give rise to a crisis of legitimacy. At this point the public can demand radical changes in the management of the school system. Lutz and Wang concluded that "the heart of the dissatisfaction theory declares that when the people are dissatisfied enough they will become politically active, and throw the rascals out."[9]

The rascals are repeatedly thrown out, but they usually return to power. Besides cartel members have an uncanny ability to clone themselves. While it is possible to elect new board members with different orientations, replacement within the cartel is seldom wholesale. There are enough remaining cartel members to control the recruitment and hiring process. The result is that bureaucratic inertia is the rule.[10] Very few individuals outside of the school activist community are able to stay within the decision-making loop over a long period of time. As the case studies in this book indicate, the cartel can defuse and deflect dissatisfactions through controlling the decision-making process. The cartel can also contain or reject interlopers. Yet black politics, with its entrepreneurial-style politicians, i.e., elected officials with distinct policy goals and a willingness to do what is necessary to accomplish them, poses new challenges and problems for this cartel.

Black Politicians and Schools

Blacks are beginning to serve on school boards to gain control over parent organizations and teacher unions and to assume high-ranking appointments.[11] To say that they dominate the school community, even in those cities in which they are a majority, is probably an exaggeration. However, significant political progress has been made. Moreover, black politicians have come under tremendous pressure because school performance has not changed under their stewardship. Blacks have come to power at a time when school governance is in transition. School boards have lost de facto control over administrators and teachers. Big city schools also face a declining tax base and accelerating racial resegregation. In addition, public schools are mired in a variety of state and federal rules which render pedagogic innovation difficult, if not impossible. As one former Detroit board of education member put it "school programs are funding driven"[12] rather than linked to any overall educational strategy. Recentralization and state receivership are real threats to this newly acquired political power over schools. Yet many blacks who are active in school politics believe that they are advancing the interests of all minorities by assuming control of schools.

The Rise of Black Power in Northern Schools

In 1935 W.E.B. DuBois asserted that "there are many public school systems in the North where Negroes are admitted and tolerated but they are not educated; they are crucified."[13] Race continues to be an issue in northern schools. De facto segregation became firmly entrenched when whites lived in cities; now schools have been resegregated as whites move to the suburbs.

Early southern black immigrants to urban centers were steered into all-black schools. On one hand, the host northern cities had no official discrimination policy; and on the other hand schools located in predominately black communities were often dumping grounds for unqualified white teachers, wornout equipment and facilities. However, northern public schools, similar to their southern counterparts, provided a major source of jobs for the emerging black middle class. Indeed, the inception of the black middle class may be traced to the need for black teachers to staff segregated school systems. In Detroit and Gary, black teachers were recruited from predominately black colleges in the South. The hiring of black teachers was thought to be an offertory buffer to those black activists demanding school integration. The participation of black parents increased with the hiring of more black staff members in the central office, and blacks became active in Parent-Teacher Associations. The 1960s saw an increase of protest activities directed toward schools.

For this study, the evolution of black involvement in school politics has been divided into four basic stages. Although these stages can be applied to northern cities in general, they are not mutually exclusive, nor do they represent exact time periods. The first stage (1955-1965) was characterized by the politics of access and recognition. Black parents wanted white-dominated boards to address their complaints and recognize their legitimacy as effective lobbyists for school betterment. They were apparently tired of being supplicants to the system. The *Brown v. Board of Education* ruling in 1954 was a turning point in the political consciousness of black parents. Not only were racially segregated schools unconstitutional; they had been found psychologically harmful to black children. Many parents were outraged that school boards would perpetuate a system which fostered this type of social isolation.

Board unwillingness to end de facto segregation triggered the mobilization of black voters to elect blacks to school boards. Alternately, black support in mayoral elections was offered in exchange for appointments to the board. Although the principal issue in northern black communities was the de facto segregation and the hiring of black teachers, blacks were saying that they wanted a stronger voice in the education of their children. Cultural isolation had bred poor learning habits, they believed. The schools could ameliorate this situation by adding supplements to the current curriculum and by integrating white and black students.

The second stage, 1965-1975, was characterized by competition and confrontation. The turbulent sixties rendered obsolete the carefully constructed coalitions of the fifties. Blacks ran against their white liberal allies for seats on the school board, claiming that they understood more clearly the learning problems of black children. White administrators' and teachers' credentials were questioned by radical community activists. These actions nurtured a nascent white flight, which began with the suburbanization of the nation and was accelerated by busing. White rejection of school integration stimulated new membership for the black activist communities. School activists were more militant and advocated curriculum changes to reflect black history. In addition, black teachers had become a visible force in the system and in the unions. The election of black mayors during this period intensified the struggle for power and representation among boards.

Many black educators interpreted the problems of black children as psychological. The dominant theme in the school reform literature and among educators was that black students were victims of cultural deprivation. The solution was to stress black history and role models. By taking these steps these educators claimed the schools could act as a surrogate for the troubled black family and provide a favorable environment for learning. Mildred Kornacker terms that new role a nurturing one, defined as a "child-centered [one] with life-adjustment orientation; reference identification with students; major concern with the affective or socio-emotional aspect of the work (the total student); belief that education should help individual growth and development."[14]

The third stage, 1975-1980, could be considered an attempt to consolidate and routinize political power. After having won seats on the school board and succeeding in appointing black superintendents, black school activists sought to control the inner workings of the central staff bureaucracy. This proved to be a difficult and time-consuming task. Aside from seeding the lower levels of the bureaucracy with minorities, blacks aspired to become the dominant voice outlining the plight of the schools. After many middle-level white central board staff members retired or otherwise acquiesced to the new regime, public schools were increasingly defined by the new leadership as multidimensional institutions seeking to extinguish the learned behavior of the black poor. Simultaneously, the ascendancy of the black middle class into school management offered teachers an opportunity to move outside the classroom and to demonstrate non-teaching skills.

The third phase also saw the full consequences of the rise of conservatism in America and tax-draining effects of white flight. The schools were increasingly populated by the children of the black poor. In this stage black administrators gained relative control over the school central office and area administrative positions. Black teachers were elected to the presidency of teacher unions. In addition, a tacit agreement developed between black mayors and teacher unions which allowed the union virtual control over school governance in exchange for support in mayoral and other municipal elections.

The current stage is characterized by fiscal crises occasioned by the loss of tax revenue and the decline of student enrollment. Blacks control the boards but not the finances. The financial problems are, in part, the result of the high cost of maintaining a large patronage system and the added expenses of creating more welfare/security services in the schools. As a result, some city schools are in some form of receivership by the state. City hall influence has increased as the mayor has become the principal lobbyist for the school board. Mayoral support is increasingly sought for millage elections. In addition, municipal police provide more services to the schools.

Since school programs are so dependent upon multiple sources of school finance, administrative sovereignty is lost in the process. Local property taxes cannot support the burden of the school system. Control is increasingly abdicated to the state bureaucracy and a variety of grant-driven programs of the federal government. The goal of the current national public school industry is to reduce local control, shift more regulatory control to state governments, and increase federal funding. There is a new alliance between school officials, unions, and supporting groups to increase administrative centralization and to rely less on local financing of schools.

Despite the Reagan and Bush Administrations' resistance to the demands of the education lobbies, school officials have been very successful in attracting money from the federal government. However, there are new problems. First, the black administrators have not maintained the image of good stewardship nurtured by their white predecessors. Part of the problem is related to their status as newcomers and the lingering racism in the general society. A second problem is the financial and educational disparity between inner city schools and suburbs, which has grown worse. White suburban politicians have been very successful in maintaining the district system of school governance with its funding disparities. With the assistance of *Milliken v. Bradley* [15] which outlawed cross-district bussing, the policy of containing black school children has been realized.[16] Simultaneously, a selective policy of attracting a limited number of black professionals to the suburbs has also been relatively successful.[17] Third, the economic instability of the remaining inner city families and neighborhoods has emerged as yet another impediment to a strong tax base for quality schools. Ironically, the decentralization experiment of the seventies, designed to disperse political power, actually created a new breed of school activists who wanted a piece of the school patronage system. The political cost of maintaining their participation (i.e., power sharing) became an additional burden for the school district. Although the activists have been partially coopted by the cartel, new legitimacy questions threaten to undo these alliances. In addition, school officials cannot stop the hemorrhaging of middle-class students from inner city school systems.

Rust-Belt City Schools

Detroit, Gary, and Newark share a common history as great magnets for blacks leaving the South in search of jobs. The cities also share experimental reforms to improve schools. The famous work-study Gary Plan of William Wist was attempted in Detroit in 1918 by Charles L. Spain, who observed it first in Gary. Despite these similarities, the school systems have different histories and possess extremely different causes of their current problems.

Economically, the three cities arose as the result of the growth of manufacturing industries—Detroit-made cars, Gary-made steel, and Newark-made beer, machine tools, and jewelry. Newark's Petro-chemicals and ports became a major industrial product after World War II. Besides becoming an insurance headquarters, Newark is best known for having New York's third airport. When these industries went into decline or shifted their assets elsewhere, the cities' economic foundation collapsed. Whites who could leave did so quickly. In the space of two decades these cities underwent a demographic transformation. Blacks and Hispanics became the dominant ethnic group. The disinvestment and depopulation was so massive that parts of these cities look like ghost towns. Table 1 shows changes in the percentage of the black population since 1940, when blacks began coming to these cities in large numbers.

Table 1. Black Percentages of Population by Decade

Year	1940	1950	1960	1970	1980	1990
Detroit	9.2	16.2	28.8	43.6	63.1	76.0
Gary	18.3	29.3	38.8	52.8	70.8	82.0
Newark	10.6	17.1	34.1	54.2	58.2	58.2

Source: U.S. Census Bureau

The increase in the black population changed the political context of each city in the late sixties. Detroit has lost 14.6% (175, 000 people) of its population since 1980. The 1990 Census also showed that Newark lost 16.4% (54, 027 people) of its population. Except for the Caribbean, Puerto Rican, Portuguese, and Ecuadorian migration to Newark, few outstate people seek these cities as a place to settle.

Each of these cities is a textbook example of corporate disinvestment with a loss of retail stores in the Central Business District and competition with surrounding communities for residents. All three cities in this study have a disproportionate percentage of a minority population and have acute problems with poverty and unemployment. Yet in these cities blacks achieved their first political successes in school politics. In the late 1970s they were able to elect black school board members and hire black school superintendents.

Black children became the majority population in the schools before the mass hiring of black teachers. The black proportion of the school population has increased because of white out-migration. Many white teachers and administrators retired, leaving the system in the hands of their younger black colleagues. However, all three school systems had evolved into organizations in which the central board staff exercised considerable control over the activities in the districts. Yet their demographic profiles, except for size, are similar.

The Detroit Public School System, created in 1842, is an excellent example of a large bureaucratic system. Today there are 271 schools: 161 elementary, 87 middle schools and 23 high schools. The system enrolls 175,469 students. Of these, 88.4% are black, 1.6% Hispanic, 9% white, and 1% other. The system has 18,000 employees, 8,000 of whom are teachers. The nature of the student population has changed radically over the last twenty years. Teachers now encounter less class and ethnic heterogeneity in their students. In 1980, 37.9% of students' families were listed below the poverty line. The estimated percentage for 1990 is 47%.[18]

The current per pupil expenditure in Detroit is $3,696 as compared with Southfield, the city's competitor for black professionals, which spends an average of $5,857 per pupil. The student-teacher ratio is 24:1 as compared to Southfield's 16:1. The District also has a 15.6 % dropout rate as compared to the overall state rate of 5.8%.[19]

The Detroit school district is governed by an elected school board. The board consists of eleven members (four at-large and seven district representatives), the majority of whom are black. In 1972 the system was decentralized into eight regional administrative districts. By 1981 so much dissatisfaction had developed, that the voters returned control to a central board. Although promoted as a cost-saving device, it was really a political move to stem the growth of political entrepreneurs in the regions. The school superintendent retained the administrative structures (i.e., boards, local school community organization, and administrative staffs) created by the decentralization experiment. He simply called them "areas" instead of regions. The new activists, mobilized by regional school politics, were encouraged to participate in Local School Community Organizations.[20]

The Gary School System, created in 1906, is the second largest employer in the city yet is a small system compared to that of most inner cities. The system employs 3,352 individuals, 1,573 of whom are teachers, and enrolls 27,052 students. The Gary school board, operating a smaller system, did not decentralize. Membership on the board has always been dominated by middle-class professionals. There are 40 schools: twenty-nine elementary, six middle schools, and five high schools. At the beginning of this study, the budget for fiscal 1988 was $93,748,862. The highest percentage of the Gary school budget revenue comes from state aide and basic grants (60.8%) and local property taxes (32%). The remaining 7% derives from interest payments, county government, and other sources.[21]

The Newark public schools, started in 1676, is one of the oldest systems in New Jersey. Newark is a middle-sized system. There are 80 schools, 58 elementary, two middle schools, seven schools for the handicapped, and thirteen senior high schools. It employs 7,506 people, 4271 of whom are teachers. The total student population is 50,791, of whom 64.2% are black, 25.5% Hispanics and 9.6% white.[22] The Newark school board, consisting of nine elected members, is a Type 2 system (i.e., an elected board). The elections are administered by the board staff. In the state of New Jersey school districts are automatically a Type 1, mayoral-appointed board unless the voters elect to switch to a Type 2 district, a district-wide elected board. In 1983 the voters of Newark switched to an elected board. I will discuss the politics surrounding this transition in detail in chapter 5.

The Research Strategy

Recently the case study approach to analyzing public policy has experienced a resurgence. This comparative approach to the study of school policy should enable us to appreciate the contextual nature of each city. To understand these cities better, we must review the history of the black regimes that govern them. I did extensive interviews with school board members, school activists, central staffs, superintendents, former mayors, and superintendents in Detroit, Gary, and Newark. Besides reading the local media coverage of schools, I read most, if not all, of the public documents, state reports, superintendent statements, and school activities reports from 1950 to 1990. With this information I was able to analyze school governance attitudes, strategies, and results. The data collected by schools in this study are not very good. Most data are in event-reporting form (i.e., concentrating on what happened rather than why) and school census counts. These data were amenable to a variety of interpretations. In attempting to capture the reality of inner city school politics, this book examines the context, major actors, events, and issues that confronted black schoolpersons and the colleagues of municipal politicians. As stated earlier, school districts are state agencies and are therefore amenable to the political culture and politics of the state.

Chapter 2 analyzes the development of Detroit schools, politics, and recurrent fiscal problems. It begins with the emergence of blacks in school politics and analyzes the effects of demographic changes within the school system.

Chapter 3 reports Gary school politics. Once known for the famous Gary Plan, the city school policy was dominated by one man for three decades. The chapter reports this history but also analyzes the modern Gary school district.

Chapter 4 examines the Newark school system, the politics of which reflect its border with New York City. As a suburb of one of the nation's largest cities (New York), it shares most of the economic difficulties of this aging metropolis. The information in this chapter relies heavily on newspaper reports. School officials in Newark are among the most difficult to interview.

Chapter 5 reviews the role of states in the development of local school policy in Indiana, Michigan, and New Jersey. Each has different economies, educational histories, and personalities involved in school politics. Local districts evolved differently in each state.

Chapter 6 analyzes the role of black mayors in school policy. I will discuss the limitations of mayoral power, particularly those regarding school policies, and its relationship to economic issues.

Chapter 7 brings together the issues of schools, labor markets, and race. The economic context of schools is critical to assessing the efficacy of the schools' relationship to their host cities. I discuss the economic conditions of the three cities.

The final chapter summarizes why school reform is so difficult to implement in these cities. The chapter raises several questions about the direction and purpose of school reform. It explains why entrenched interests have been so successful at resisting attempts to reform schools.

NOTES

1. See Jonathan Kozol, *Savages Inequalities* (New York: Crown Publications, 1992).

2. National Center for Educational Statistics, *The Condition of Education* (Washington, D.C.: U.S. Department of Education, 1994).

3. See Douglas Yates, *The Ungovernable City* (Cambridge: MIT Press, 1978).

4. Nathan Grundstein, "Future Manpower for Urban Managers," in *Emerging Patterns of Urban Administration,* F. Gerald Brown and Thomas Murphy, ed. (Lexington: D.C. Heath, 1974).

5. David Tyack, "Public School Reform: Policy Talk and Institutional Practice," *American Journal of Education* 100 (1991): 1-19.

6. See Clarence Stone, *Regime Politics: Governing Atlanta, 1946-1988* (Lawrence: University of Kansas Press, 1989).

7. See Frank Lutz and Lee Yan Wang, *Public Participation in Local School Districts* (Lexington: Lexington Books).

8. Stone, op. cit.

9. Frank Lutz and Lee-Yan Wang, "Predicting Public Dissatisfaction: A Study of School Board Member Defeat," *Educational Administration Quarterly* 23 (February, 1988), p. 75.

10. I thank Joe Stewart for this insight.

11. Kenneth J. Meier and Robert E. England, "Black Representation and Educational Policy: Are They Related?," *American Political Science Review* 78 (June 1984): 392-403.

12. Interview with Thomas Stallworth, August 1, 1989.

13. W.E.B. DuBois, "Does the Negro Need Separate Schools," *Journal of Negro Education* 5 (Summer 1935), p. 328.

14. Mildred Kornacker, "The Ethnic Teacher in Urban Classrooms: Differential Orientations to the Teacher Role," *Education and Urban Society*, 1, (May, 1969), p. 249.

15. Milliken v. Bradley , 418 U.S. 717 (1974).

16. Joseph Radelet, "Stillness at the Detroit's Racial Divide: A Perspective on Detroit's School Desegregation Court Order-1970-1989," *The Urban Review* 23 (September 1991): 173-190.

17. John Stahura, "Suburban Development, Black Suburbanization and the Civil Rights Movement Since WWII," *American Sociological Review* 51 (1986): 131-144.

18. *Vantage "21"* Detroit Public School Strategic Plan: Internal Analysis Data (Detroit Board of Education), March, 1989, p. 3.

19. Data from Detroit Board of Education, 1989.

20. Interview with Dr. Arthur Jefferson, April 17, 1990.

21. Data from Gary Board of Education, 1989.

22. Data from Newark Board of Education, 1989.

CHAPTER 2

Detroit School Politics

Created in 1842, the Detroit School District started with a population of 9,102.[1] Located in each of the city's seven wards, school administrators were very tightly linked to the political system. The only exceptions were the separate city-wide schools for blacks in the black community. The first all black school in Detroit had thirty-six students. At the time the city had 193 black residents. In 1868 the Michigan Supreme Court ended *de jure* segregated schools. The entire nineteenth century history of Detroit schools was one of encroachment of political machines and patronage.

Jeffrey Mirel, who started his review of Detroit school history at the year 1907, found that school politics had everything from textbook purchase scandals to board election shenanigans.[2] The last and most notable political boss of schools was Wade Martindale, superintendent from 1887 to 1912. Martindale was able to keep the reformers at bay because he introduced a progressive curriculum and used patronage to retain political support in the city wards. His firing in 1912 was the first of a series of reform victories that included elimination of the election of board members by wards in 1916 and the triumph of the first reform slate in school history in 1917. School reformers were able to take control of the board after they formed a coalition with municipal reformers and the Protestant clergy. The surgery to remove partisan politics from the school system was quite invasive but failed to ferret out all of the cancer.

Black children started to make their presence felt in the school system as early as 1920. The twenties were considered the finest years of Detroit schools.[3] The Depression ended this era, but southern black immigrants were still being pushed north. By 1940 there were nearly 150,000 blacks in the city. Yet the biggest increase was to come during World War II when the 1950 census showed a 200% increase in the black population, bringing the number up to 298,875. In 1960 blacks represented 29% of the city population but black children were 45.8% of the school population. Most of these black newcomers lived in designated enclaves, and their children attended predominately black schools. De facto segregation emerged as the unofficial policy of the school system. Over the years as the city population grew with the expansion of the automobile industry, schools responded to that growth. Detroit, the largest district in Michigan, was a predominately white system until the 1960s. After the 1967 riot and the resultant white flight, the district evolved into a black majority school district.

Detroit, until recently, could provide jobs for a majority of its high school graduates. As the automobile industry declined, the city labor market followed in its wake. The loss of jobs has led to a population decline. Between 1970 and 1980, there was a 20.5% decrease in population, the majority of which was white. According to the 1990 census count, the city is 76% black. White flight has been followed by middle-class black flight. Economists and planners[4] have noted that Detroit is a prime example of disinvestment in Rust-Belt cities. The school system has reflected these sweeping changes in population and economic base.

The Emergence of Black School Politicians

The black presence in the school system emerged in the 1950 census. Blacks represented 16.2% of the total population but a larger percentage of the school population. Blacks began agitating for a seat on the school board in the early fifties and succeeded in electing Dr. Remus Robinson, a physician, in 1955. This was one year after the famous *Brown v. Board of Education* ruling, which outlawed de jure segregation in southern states. The psycho-sociological reasoning behind the decision included the notion that black children were damaged by segregated schools. Black leaders thought that the psychological damage could occur in the de facto segregated schools in Detroit. Instead of retaining black schools, they wanted the administration to end segregation of students and instead hire more black teachers and administrators throughout the school system. I call this stage of black involvement in schools, the politics of access and recognition.

Members of the Detroit Board of Education tried to appease blacks by reassuring them of their commitment to school integration. In 1956 the board passed the Fair Employment Practice Regulations. In addition, Superintendent Samuel Brownwell appointed the Citizens Advisory Committee on School Needs, 270 members strong, to hold hearings on needed changes in the system. The members were selected from school activists in the eight administrative districts. Chaired by George Romney, President of American Motors, the Committee surveyed the entire system. A subcommittee of the Committee, which included black civil rights leaders, was able to document the discriminatory practices of school system. Although the report called for curriculum reform, it had little to say as to how to desegregate Detroit schools, except suggesting that attendant boundary lines be drawn without regard to race. The report was well received by the black community and provided the board with support to launch a successful millage renewal election.[5]

Although the 1960 Census showed that blacks constituted 29% of the population, the school system remained segregated. The dominant controversy in educational circles became busing to achieve integration. In 1962 the Citizens' Advisory Committee on Equal Education Opportunity, chaired by Judge Nathan Kaufman and Dr. Robert M. Frehse, found that 75 of the city's 273 schools were all white, 29 predominately white, 8 all-black, and 70 predominately black. The reports endorsed neighborhood schools but did not recommend total integration. They suggested a scheme in which some blacks would be allowed to attend integrated schools.[6] The next year blacks become the majority in the school system.

The board and superintendents continued to state publicly that they were committed to end segregation. However, no changes were made. A group of black lawyers calling themselves Citizens for Jones School Committee filed a race discrimination suit against the system. The suit was withdrawn after the superintendent made stronger promises to dismantle the segregated Detroit School System. In 1958 the board elected its only black member, Dr. Robinson, as president. In the school board election of 1958, two incumbent board members declared themselves reformers and joined with Roy Stevens to form the second major reform slate in Detroit's history. Mirel cites 1949 to 1964 as the rise of the liberal-black coalition in Detroit school politics. He attributes this rise to power to the shift from class to race politics.[7]

The Court and De Facto Segregation

A good example of the racialization of school politics was the Sherrill case. In 1962 a group of parents at the Sherrill schools filed a suit against the Detroit schools for maintaining de facto segregated schools. Although the evidence and various citizens' reports supported their claims, the board denied that it created segregated schools. The Sherrill action was the result of the growing influence of black nationalists in Detroit. Rev. Albert Cleage was leader of the parent group, the Sherrill School Parent Committee. They also had the support of the newly formed Trade Union Leadership Council, a black political organization. However, the NAACP leadership decided not to support the Sherrill suit.

Cleage used this refusal to support the Sherrill suit as an example of the failure of the so-called establishment oriented black leadership. Cleage and his organization Group of Advanced Leadership (GOAL) emerged for a brief period as players in school politics. Black militants found their way into the various internecine battles of Detroit school politics. After two years the Sherrill suit was dropped, in part, because the 1964 school election restored faith in the labor-liberal coalition.

Faith in Labor-Liberal Coalition

Formed in 1949, as the so-called liberal-labor coalition's Serve our Schools Committee, the coalition had elected most of the candidates it endorsed. In the 1964 school board election, the teacher's union, the Detroit Federation of Teachers, sponsored its first slate of candidates called the Save Our Schools Team. The candidates included Peter Grylls, Abe L. Zwerdling and Rev. Darneau Stewart, a black man. Zwerdling, a former United Automobile Workers (UAW) union staff lawyer, had been persuaded to run for the board at the urging of Walter Reuther, President of the UAW. The slate was elected, and Stewart became the second elected black school board member. Mirel asserted that "on paper, no school board elected in Detroit was better equipped to deal with severe racial and class conflict than the one that took office on July 1, 1965."[8] This election established a pro-integration majority on the board. The triumph of these social activists did not mean the end of the school cartel grip on power. When they tried to change school policy, they discovered that central bureaucracy was entrenched.

The black community became impatient and created an Ad Hoc Committee Concerned with Equal Educational Opportunity. The members included Rev. William Ardrey, Richard Austin, Rev. Nicholas Hood, Alvin Loving, Horace Sheffield, Rev. Wadworth, Charles Wells, and Coleman Young. This committee demanded implementation of the recommendations for inclusion of blacks in the apprenticeships of Detroit schools.[9] This group joined the NAACP in criticizing school system's hiring practices. These black leaders had to speak out. Otherwise, grass-roots leaders like Rev. Cleage would accuse them of collaborating with the forces that kept the schools segregated. Despite their complaints, the schools continued to operate in the old ways.

Zwerdling became a dominant force on the board and spearheaded the fight to oust Superintendent Sam Brownwell. Norman Drachler was appointed superintendent, and the board appointed Arthur Johnson, a former NAACP official and deputy director of the Michigan Civil Rights Commission, as deputy superintendent. Now the system could boast a highly visible black board official (Johnson) with civil rights credentials in the superintendent's office. Johnson had served on the Citizens Advisory Committee on School Needs and the Citizens' Advisory

Committee on Equal Education Opportunity. The team of Drachler and Johnson's began to move forward with attempts to integrate the system. Pilo describes Drachler's integration effort as "unrivaled in any northern city."[10] As evidence he cites:

> From 1966 to 1970, the proportion of black school instructional staff rose from 31.7% to 41.2% (an increase of one third), and the proportion of black noninstructional staff rose from 41% to 58.2% (an increase of better than two fifths). All this occurred while the proportion of the student body which is black increased by only one eighth (from 56.7% to 63.8%), and the same time as the number of all-white schools in the Detroit system declined from 22 to 11.[11]

These changes were significant but they were too little and too late. Detroit schools had become a target for widespread discontent in the black community. Despite Drachler and Johnson's efforts to change student assignment patterns, black resentment grew toward the schools. Widick cites the deterioration of public schools as a source of racial tension.

> The deterioration of the Detroit public school system was another sore point in the Negro community. The increase in the black population from 30 to 40 per cent of the total population created a de facto segregation in the schools. The number of children rose by 50,000 adding to the already overcrowded conditions. And the 50 per cent drop-out rate among black youth is hardly surprising when one considers that the white teachers and principals were totally unprepared— either by education or experience—to handle black students. "Baby sitting'" rather than education, and discipline rather than influence over youth, became the frequent pattern of work for the frightened or helpless schoolteachers.[12]

The school crisis pales in comparison with the general alienation of black Detroiters. Unemployment, poverty, and poor police/community relations led to what Widick called an earthquake.[13] In July 1967 the city experienced a major riot that required federal troops to quell. This event accelerated more white flight. In the aftermath of the riot, the Detroit High School Study Commission declared "our high schools are appallingly inadequate—a disgrace to the community and a tragedy to the thousands of young men and women whom we compel and cajole to sit in them."[14] By the end of the decade black political leaders, both traditional and militant grass-roots types, had grown into an important force in city politics. In 1969 blacks and their labor allies tried to elect a black mayor, only to be rebuffed by a white voter bloc.[15]

Meanwhile, the idea of community control of schools gripped the imagination of many black activists. The interest in community control came at a time when the numbers were on the side of the black community. Reverend Albert Cleage, pastor of the Central United Church of Christ, formed the Inner City Parents' Council to promote more community control for blacks. He was joined by Black State Representative James Del Rio, who introduced the first decentralization bill in the Michigan Assembly. The Del Rio Bill would have divided the system into 16 autonomous mini-systems. Since Cleage and Del Rio were not members of either the public school community or the cartel, the Del Rio bill was denounced by the every school interest group in the city and also by the school board.

Decentralize to Desegregate?

Many school districts around the nation were experimenting with a decentralized school administration. The Detroit school board, with the assistance of a Ford Foundation grant of $360,000, began studying the concept of decentralization for the city. Zwerdling, then President of the School Board, become convinced that decentralization could serve to integrate the school system. He publicly announced his intentions before a national audience of school administrators. He lamented "no one who has come to our public meetings on decentralization is interested in integration. Everyone wants segregation so they will be assured a little piece of control."[16] Presumably Zwerdling did not include black leaders in his description of "everyone."

Black groups saw community control as a "black power" goal. A city-wide black group calling itself Citizens for Community Control held a conference on community control and endorsed community control as the salvation of the Detroit schools. In 1968 Andrew Perdue, a community control advocate, was elected to the board. Perdue's election represented a show of political muscle for the Cleage group. More community groups and churches were mobilized to push for community control of schools. Community activists promoted community control as the only way to wrestle the system away from the white dominated central board staff.

Again state legislation was needed to divide the schools into regions. In the summer of 1969, the state legislature passed a decentralization act championed by State Senator Coleman Young, the future mayor of Detroit. Governor Milliken signed the bill into law. The new law called for eight quasi-autonomous regions. It seemed to some that the years of school centralization had come to an end. For the first time in history blacks finally controlled the schools in their neighborhoods. Young had to appease members of the school cartel in order to end their opposition to decentralization. Mirel observed:

> In fact, Young had included two provisions in the bill
> that sharply restricted the actual power of the regional
> boards in order to get the board and the DFT to end
> their opposition to decentralization. The first of these
> two provisions was that regional boards had to operate
> under guildelines established by the central board; the
> second was that the "rights of retirement, tenure,
> seniority and of any other benefits of any employee
> transferred to regional school district or between
> regional school districts . . . shall not be abrogated,
> diminished or impaired." In other words, the Young
> bill protected some of the most important prerogatives
> of the central board and maintained the collective
> bargaining arrangements recently won by the DFT.
> Without these provisions, the bill had no chance
> of passage.[17]

The Detroit school cartel thought it had the decentralization under its control. They did not anticipate the reactions of whites to this change in policy and what effect it would have on school board election politics.

The New School Electoral Politics

Despite the fact that the school population was 64% black, whites still held the voting majority on the school board. Because of community control rhetoric and the fears of whites, voting for regional seats was divided along racial lines. Blacks still did not have the votes to control the four major school regions. Some members of the black community, led by the NAACP, demanded guarantees of integrated schools in the decentralization plan. Zwerdling created a plan which called for integrated and decentralized regions. To implement the plan, it was necessary to employ extensive busing. Since Zwerdling and his supporters did not have enough votes on the board, they lost the vote and a revised busing plan was drawn up by Superintendent Drachler. The board adopted the plan. The newspapers printed a copy of the plan, and the resulting outcry triggered a white parent protest. They organized the Committee for Better Education, boycotted the schools, and called for a recall election of the white liberals on the board. They also confronted Zwerdling and his cohorts at the board meeting, demanding repeal of the integration plan.

The state legislature tried to defuse the controversy by overwhelmingly passing a bill to repeal the decentralization law. Senator Young called it "capitulation to blind prejudice."[18] Young began work on a new decentralization law without an integration plan. The law was passed without specific boundaries for the eight new regions. Each region had a five-member elected board. The board member with the largest number of votes in the regional election would become chairman and would represent the region on the central board. The new 1970 law, Public Act #48, required boards to send children from the district to the school closest to their home. Part of the Act also required a referendum on decentralization and provided that a commission draw the regional lines for Detroit. This act maintained the budget, collective bargaining, and construction at the central board level. The

Appeals Court later suspended the no-busing provision of the act. The new bill did not appease the mobilized members of the Citizen's Committee for Better Education. They were able to get enough signatures to get the recall question on the ballot. With only a 23% turnout of voters, they were successful in removing liberal white board members Zwerdling and Peter Grylls, and black member Reverend Stewart. Zwerdling had repeatedly supported integrated schools during his tenure as board president and drew most of the heat from white parents. The recall was a triumph of white parental power.

Eight regions were created, and whites were able to capture control of six. Blacks only controlled two districts, despite holding a majority of black students in at least six districts. Attempts to draw the line so that blacks would capture four districts failed. Blacks also lost seats on the central board. Patrick McDonald, Zwerdling's nemesis on the board, was elected president. Drachler was forced to resign. C.T. Clotfelter concluded that "in fighting integration during the recall campaign, whites who had opposed decentralization for two years suddenly embraced community control as they realized that segregated regions would protect them forever from the threat of integration that the Zwerdling plan had posed."[19]

The schools remained relatively segregated. In 1971 the U.S. Supreme Court, with *Swann v. Charlotte-Mecklenburg County Board of Education*, held that busing was only permissible if used to correct old segregated systems. Busing could not be used to correct de facto segregation. Detroit, like most northern cities, had relatively rigid race boundaries for housing. Yet there were attempts to achieve integration through busing despite the fact that there were not enough white students left to truly integrate the system. The only available pool of white students lived in the surrounding suburbs.

The board adopted a metropolitan desegregation plan involving the tri-county area. The court agreed to the plan and the stage was set for extensive cross-district busing. This policy was thwarted by the U.S. Supreme Court in *Milliken v. Bradley*, in which the court outlawed cross-district busing.[20] Consequently, black children were virtually locked into the increasingly segregated Detroit system. School administrators turned their attention to integrating teachers and school workforce. By 1975 black teachers made up 51% of the teacher staff and 44% of the administrative staff.

The system's decentralization era was a turbulent one. Like decentralization in other cities, the reforms did not provide more parent access to schools but rather more jobs for administrators. The impact on school performance was nebulous. A consensus began building that the experiment was not working and was a waste of resources.[21] The conflict was also a clear example of the second stage of black involvement, the politics of competition and confrontation.

Before the cartel could move against decentralization, it needed to defuse the racial politics around community control. Something dramatic needed to be done to restore the public confidence in schools. In 1974 the board attempted to establish a residency requirement for all employees. The union took the board to court, which ruled that the residency requirement was a bargainable issue. The ruling was a major defeat for the board. Having lost this issue, the board searched for a new way to reassert itself and restore public confidence. In 1975 the board hired its first black superintendent, Arthur Jefferson. The appointment was greeted as a great leap forward, and it was hoped that the black constituency would support future millage elections now that the schools had new leadership.

The Election of Coleman Young

The 1973 election of Coleman A. Young as Detroit's first black mayor represented a triumph of black politics in the Motor City.[22] Young had been a labor organizer, insurance salesman, and state senator. As state senator he had taken a keen interest in school politics and was consulted by education lobbyists regarding issues that faced the Detroit school system. At the time of Young's election the city was 46% black. However, blacks had vastly improved their voter registration rates since the close loss of a mayoral campaign in 1969. Young campaigned on the theme of fairness and more city jobs for blacks. He promised to end an anti-crime unit called STRESS (i.e., Stop Robbers, Enjoy Safe Streets). Young was also known as a friend to Detroit schools.

In Coleman Young's first reelection bid he came out forcefully for a 3 mill increase. Young also asserted that the millage increase "... is the principal issue of this campaign. A candidate who talks about education but doesn't have the guts to take a stand would make a poor excuse for a mayor."[23] The candidate to whom he referred was Councilman Ernie Brown. Brown had been conducting a character campaign against the mayor, a strategy that failed.[24]

Young also went on record as questioning the use of the property tax as a method of raising revenue for the schools. He wanted to substitute a graduated income tax for the residential property tax. In the same interview he also suggested that schools be placed under the aegis of City Hall or else that the school superintendent be elected.[25] The board President, Carolyn Kennedy, immediately objected to the idea of schools being a part of city government. She replied, "I don't think the schools should be made more of a political football than they are now."[26]

The Jefferson Era

The Court held in *Milliken v. Bradley* that cross district busing was not an appropriate remedy for de jure segregation in districts. The court then ordered the desegregation of Detroit schools. In 1975 Judge DeMascio took the case after the death of Judge Roth. With assistance of Wilbur Cohen, Francis Koeppel, and John Finger, officials from the U.S. Office of Education, he ordered changes in teacher and student assignments, community participation and the establishment of a monitoring commission. Black children, now constituting 75% of districts, bore the burden of being bused. In 1977 the U.S. Supreme Court upheld the DeMascio busing plan, and the state of Michigan was forced to pay for some of the transportation costs. White flight reached pandemic proportions. Black children were being bused to schools with only a tiny minority of white students. School desegregation had failed, and black children were virtually locked into the increasingly segregated Detroit system.

The hiring of its first black superintendent, Arthur Jefferson, came in the midst of these busing rulings. Nonetheless, Dr. Jefferson's tenure began on an upbeat note. He knew many of the city politicians and labor leaders. Dr. Jefferson had no problem presiding over an increasingly black district. He characterized his reception. "Detroit had moved further ahead (than other cities). There was a more balanced staff, teacher and administrators. There were more blacks in important management position, setting the stage internally for me."[27]

His task was to improve the performance of the system and make it more amenable to rising demands for more neighborhood participation. The other task, although not articulated, was to recentralize the school system. Jefferson was perfect for the job. As a former regional superintendent, he was familiar with administrative problems of the regional boards. Before Jefferson and the recentralizers could move, they needed more time to consolidate power.

The strategy adopted by the recentralizer was to shift attention away from integration and decentralization. In 1977 Jefferson promulgated what he called *A Call to Action*, a challenge to improve school performance and reform the curriculum. However, the new superintendent's plan influenced the political discourse in school politics for a short time. School watchers were more interested in the confusion and contradiction of the various regional leaders. By 1981 the cartel had sowed enough doubt that decentralization had few defenders. The state legislature got no resistance when it passed a law which allowed the Detroit voters to vote out decentralization. Voters voted overwhelming to end this experiment in power sharing.

Power to the School Center Building

The decade of the eighties became the recentralization era. The debacle of the New York City's Ocean Hill-Brownsville schools served to undermine the foundations' plans for selling the idea of decentralization as a solution to urban educational woes. The teacher unions, both nationally and locally, stood steadfast against the concept. Detroit decentralization efforts left most people disappointed. In the name of efficiency and coordination, most administrative functions reverted again to the School Centers Building. No one was more disappointed with its failure than its sponsor, Senator Young.

> It was community control. It was direct participation in the school system. It gave the community the right to determine teachers and administrators. It gave them a hands-on say about policy. It was very unfortunate that it was dissolved. They returned it to the big debating riot at the central board.[28]

Recentralization was not without its perils. Many activists created by the decentralization movement now competed with each other for new jobs and influence. In the 1982 election for the central board, control of the board went to newly mobilized local activists. The thirteen-member central board, which included representatives from the eight regional boards, was reduced to eleven members (four at-large seats and seven districts). This election marked the end of the consolidation period for black involvement in school politics. Dr. Jefferson was ensconced in the superintendent's office, and in 1981 John Elliot, a black man, was elected president of Detroit Federation of Teachers.

The New School Politics

The 1982 election shaped school politics for a decade. After that election the cartel leadership had to spend enormous energy mediating internecine political campaigns among cartel members. Clara Rutherford, the vice-president of the Board, was challenged by three opponents. George Bell ran for the seat in Region #1, and Gloria Cobbin ran against fellow board member Ida Murray. Carolyn Kennedy was challenged by Carrie Holloway, who was then vice-president of the Detroit Council of the Parents, Teachers and Students Association (PTSO). George Vaughn ran against former regional member Bertha Kaminsky for the Region #4 seat. Harold Murdock campaigned against Herman Davis, a former board member. Board elections had become a Hobbsean war—all against all.

The 1982 election results demonstrated the shift from insider to outsider politics. Incumbent Joan Gacki beat Mary Borowski for the Region #6 seat , which was predominantly white and working class. Rosemary Osborne beat Alonzo Bates for the region #7 seat. George Bell, who had previously been ousted as Wayne County Community College President, was deposed as president by the newly elected board. Harold Murdock became the new President of the Board.

By the 1986 election the infighting on the board became public. Cartel socialization was successful in maintaining the status quo in school policy but was not able to maintain decorum among board members. Board President Mudock resigned after allegations of kickbacks in a school milk vendor contract. His petition signatures for reelection were declared invalid by the County Clerk's office. This precipitated an acute crisis for the board as the newspapers began unprecedented muckraking of board member activity.

A Crisis of Confidence

The political reputation of the incumbent board members was undermined in 1987 when it was disclosed that the system was $160 million in debt, and, nevertheless, board members were abusing their travel vouchers and going to meetings in chauffeured cars. Complaints of excessive spending for travel and use of chauffeur-driven cars became the leading topic in the media and on the streets of Detroit.

In November 1987 State Treasurer Robert Bowman ordered an end to chauffeur-driven cars before he would attempt to sell $78 million dollars of the school district's short-term notes. The board promised action upon his request but did not enact any restrictive policies on cars.

The state treasurer reacted angrily to newspaper reports of continued use of chauffeured cars and took action in May of 1988 to hold up the sale of $30 million of short-term notes. Without the sale, there would be no money to pay teacher salaries. Board President Gloria Cobbin attacked Bowman. "I think it's racist. We challenged the state's authority to impose these restriction on how we run our school system."[29] Cobbin was joined by Mayor Young. The mayor observed, "I don't think that it is his [the treasurer's] function. He is not the state superintendent of schools. State money and state authorization should not be used as a stick."[30] Board member Osborne, who was not up for reelection, added, "I am not backing down. I don't think he has the authority to do this. This is a legitimate expense. I only use the board drivers for board related activities. He would be depriving my district of representation because I am unable to drive at night."[31]

Since Detroit Board members are not paid a regular salary, a tradition has been established of expanding board members' in-kind benefits and perks. These included sponsored trips to frequent school and educational conferences and the privilege of being chauffeured while conducting board business. The media reported on the travel and use of chauffeured cars as examples of board members' ostentatious behavior in the face of the schools' growing debt.

This crisis was precipitated not over some new method of teaching or de facto segregation, but over an issue the so-called man-in-the street could understand. Board members were portrayed as spoiled, arrogant, and out of touch with the people. There were calls for the removal of all incumbents. New recall challenges were launched by People to Open Schools and Parents for Better Schools. These organizations started a petition to recall George Bell, who had been already replaced as president of the board. Parents for Better Schools also wanted to recall Bell, Gloria Cobbin, then president, and Clara Rutherford, the first black woman elected to the board. They focused their protest on the use of chauffeured cars by board members in the face of the deficit. The recall movement represented a serious challenge for the school cartel because it invited new actors and interests into the policy arena. The reaction to the scandal is a classic example of the dissatisfaction theory. Professor Lutz and Wang observed:

> Dissatisfaction theory postulates that, as dissatisfaction increases in a school district, more challengers run against incumbents and more incumbents choose to retire rather than risk defeat at the polls. . . . As public dissatisfaction with policy occurs, the incumbent board may refuse to run to accommodate the demands generated by dissatisfaction. As dissatisfaction continues, it becomes likely that the incumbent will not win. These events encourage political candidates to challenge incumbents, and may result in incumbent defeat, superintendent turnover, and policy change.[32]

Considerable dissatisfaction existed within the school cartel as well as with the general public. Signs of a serious revolt from parents and the non-activist community were ominous. Removing all board members and replacing them with community activists, particularly those activists not sanctioned by the school community, could mean loss of control and status for the members of the school board. This prospect, never publicly articulated, caused a variety of reactions among the city's political elite.

The chauffeured car controversy had exposed the real issue of the campaign—the mismanagement of the district's finances. A former and frustrated board member who left the board before this controversy began gave an example of the mismanagement.

> When I was on the board there was no inventory control. People just ordered supplies. You would be asked what happened to the stuff you ordered before. What about all the gym equipment? They (staff) just order new stuff. There was no investigation. There was no accountability. The warehouse was jammed full of stuff. If you needed the stuff bad, you couldn't get it.[33]

No one was willing to accept the blame for the lingering deficit. Moreover, board members viewed the attack by the state treasurer as a ploy to embarrass them publicly. State officials were still unhappy about the board's settlement of a strike by increasing teacher salaries with no plans to raise money to pay for the contract. Even the mayor had criticized the settlement as fiscally unsound. He opined that "they (union) were selfish."[34] Coming off a successful millage increase election three years ago, the board was confident that the public would again vote to increase the millage. The board believed that it had the union commitment to work for a four mill renewal, a six mill increase and a bond sale to pay off the $160,000,000 debt. Since 1975 the board had tremendous success in selling millage increases to Detroit voters. They would campaign heavily in the black neighborhoods, promising better school performance for their children and freedom from state intervention.

In addition to the fiscal crisis and charges of unethical behavior, the superintendent's performance became part of the controversy. Dr. Arthur Jefferson had become a fixture in the school system. Jefferson was a consensus builder and sensitive to the needs of the various political factions in the city. The public was generally satisfied with its first and only black superintendent until the newspaper accounts of financial mismanagement. Polls indicated a loss of confidence in Jefferson's leadership. Throughout the year newspaper polls indicated widespread dissatisfaction with board members, superintendents, student performance, and school safety. The tightly knit inner circle of the school board members began to unravel after well-publicized allegations of incompetence, mismanagement, and corruption.

The political fires had been smoldering under the Schools Center Building (the administrative board's office) for several years. Most employees and board members had learned to survive in the caldron of school politics. School officials seemed to be enjoying Teflon careers. They had seemed oblivious to charges of mismanagement, miseducation, and misrepresentation for over a decade. In school elections no one took seriously community activists, claims of corruption and cover-ups of the problems at the School Center Building. Consequently, when a grass-roots movement to dump incumbents was launched in the spring of 1987, incumbents were not worried.

Interest Group Reactions

The recall effort was quickly recognized as a threat to the array of interest groups involved in public education. Detroit Federation of Teachers President Elliott was repeatedly asked to comment on the various reports circulating about the tenure of the Superintendent Jefferson. His hesitancy to speculate on Dr. Jefferson's situation was viewed by a few reporters as an invitation to continue to delve into the apparent failures of the entire system. Several newspapers started muckraking about the activities of board members. New Detroit, Inc., an urban advocacy organization, had its President S. Martin Taylor issue an unusually strong criticism of the board. "I do not believe the board has been effective. It appears that board members place their own well being ahead of the children. The trips and chauffeured cars, in the face of layoffs, are outrageous."[35] A newspaper poll found widespread dissatisfaction with the school system, and two-thirds of respondents rated Superintendent Jefferson only fair as an administrator.[36] In May of 1987, Dr. Jefferson's contract was renewed automatically under the state education code, which required 90-days notice before terminating a superintendent. Most of the Board members confessed ignorance of the law, prompting Taylor to observe: "If anyone had any doubts about the mind boggling irresponsibility of the school board, the last few days should clear that up."[37] Tom Turner, Secretary-Treasurer of the Michigan AFL-CIO and a major black leader in the city, observed "There is a cancer in this system as it relates to the lack of education. It is time to stop treating that with a band aid approach. Now is the time for major surgery."[38] It became clear to the public that the board would undergo major membership changes.

The real purpose behind the public statement of indignation began to surface in the early stages of the recall effort. The recall effort was spearheaded by the cartel and its allies and the so-called grass-roots community leadership. The recall movement got off to a good start after a summer of voter registration. The grass-roots community concentrated its recall efforts on a specific incumbent, George Bell. People to Open Schools (POP) collected 10,227 names. They needed only 7,692 to put the issue on the ballot. However, 3, 136 signers lived outside Bell's district. The petitions were disallowed. POP was advised to wait for the 1988 primary election rather than push for a special election. In agreeing to delay the recall effort, POP lost the momentum and the spotlight to other interest groups. The action now shifted to the upcoming school board primary. The primary saw better organized and funded interest groups take center stage in the reform movement.

The 1988 Primary

Despite seemingly endless charges against the incumbent school board members Clara Rutherford, Marie Blackmon, Alonzo Bates, and Marie Jackson-Randolph, they decided to seek reelection. George Bell resigned his seat and Gloria Cobbin became board president. Thirty-two individuals filed for seats on the board, doubling the number of candidates from 1984. Notable among them were Joseph Blanding (who had been defeated in 1986), Bennett Nowicki (a school gadfly) and Frederick Long, an academic. However, the main opposition was the group HOPE. It included Frank Hayden, a city employee (who also had been a losing candidate in 1986), Larry Patrick (a lawyer) and David Olmstead (also a lawyer and the only white member of the coalition). Olmstead had served on the Michigan Commission on School Finance and was considered an expert on school finance. This reform took the first letter of each of those members' surname and called itself HOPE. The "E" stood for education.

The HOPE Campaign

The HOPE coalition at first glance seem to be a classic reform organization. According to Horrace Sheffield, executive director of Detroit Association of Black Organizations (DABO), the idea for HOPE's interracial coalition evolved from one of its subgroup called Groups of Organized Detroiters for Quality Education (GOOD), started by long-time labor activist Horace Sheffield.[39] Lawrence Patrick and James Trent were co-chairmen of GOOD, an interracial group of 40 members, created to elect an "effective school board." The primary aim was to work for quality education in Detroit. A closer examination revealed that none of the candidates was a pure outsider. Frank Hayden had been a candidate for a board seat in 1982 and was a major parent leader in his child's elementary school. He had led the fight to install lights in the school's playing field over the objection of the school bureaucracy and was somewhat of a hero in his community. As stated above, Olmstead had been member of the Michigan Commission on School Finance. Joseph Blanding was active in the labor movement.

The group came under attack immediately for not having a woman on the ticket. Hayden admitted that the coalition had attempted to recruit Kay Everett, an incumbent board member not up for reelection, as the final letter for HOPE. This outreach to Everett failed and later proved to be a minor embarrassment to HOPE's reform credentials.

Joseph Blanding's name was added to the HOPE team after he survived the runoff. A deal was made with the UAW to include Blanding. Labor understood the importance of reform and wanted to be seen as supporting the goals of HOPE. This alliance with labor allowed HOPE to tap into the considerable organizing skills and financial resources of the union. In addition, the HOPE team had captured the imagination of middle-class blacks and reportedly received financial support from individuals living outside the city of Detroit.

The HOPE organization consisted of two paid staff members and about 300-400 volunteers. Their campaign manager, Hanson Clark, was a political appointee in the Wayne County Executive Office. The press person, Erma Clark, was the press secretary to County Executive Ed McNamara. The campaign had a finance director (Michele Edwards) and a full-time administrator who had offices in one of the city's major law firms (Miller, Canfield, Paddock & Stone).

There was no official leader of HOPE. The coalition campaign was designed to be a campaign of equals. Despite having the services of veteran campaign managers, the coalition campaigning was highly uncoordinated and fragmented. In retrospect, their amateurish appearance probably helped them politically. The campaign, funded by heavyweights in both political parties, outspent the incumbents. The record showed that the coalition raised over $100,000. The largest contributors were Max Fisher, a Republican ($1,000) and the Detroit Federation of Teachers ($5,000). The rest of the contributions were in the $25 dollar range.

The theme of HOPE was sometimes called "local school empowerment," which was roughly translated as allowing local school principals more autonomy in school policy. Some described the local school empowerment campaign as decentralization of decision-making without regionalization. The literature of the HOPE team described the purpose of school-based management.

> School-Based Management provides schools with greater decision-making authority through a process in which the principal establishes regular and meaningful opportunities for representatives of students, parents, community administrators, instructional and non-instructional school staff to have input into the selection of areas and /or problems which are addressed and to suggest solutions or strategies to be used. This is done in an atmosphere of mutual trust and respect and under the leadership of the principal who is responsible for making decisions based upon the recommendations of the school's constituents.[40]

This official definition contains several significant points. First, it assumes that principals wanted more control over the management of school facilities. Because they were not trained as facility managers, most principals would prefer such functions to remain in the hands of the central administration. Second, others may not want to share the newly-acquired power with teachers and the community. According to Ed Simpkin, a former Dean of Education at Wayne State, "most principals do not want the power to let contracts to fix the roof. They are more interested in curriculum matters."[41]

School-based management was a major HOPE proposal, but the campaign was about the behavior of sitting board members. Osborne, mentioned earlier, stated publicly "I am using a driver; I will continue to do so unless I'm ordered by the governor (not to)."[42] The record showed a major increase in the cost of travel to school board conventions. Between July 1, 1985, and April 1986, board members Bell, Bates, Rutherford, and Cobbin spent over $41,000 of the total $52,000 travel funds allocated to the board.[43]

The second election issue was the deficit. There were several estimates given for the school deficit. The superintendent and his deputy for finance could not pinpoint the actual figure. The State Board of Education established a task force to review school finances. The consensus deficit was placed at $100,000, 000. Rumors had circulated that teacher layoffs were imminent. Superintendent Jefferson also suggested that several buildings be closed. The most frightening rumor was that there was not enough money to complete the school year.

Local school empowerment was lost in the charges and countercharges of unethical behavior. The HOPE slate attacked the judgment and ethics of all incumbents. Nevertheless, the incumbent group, with the exception of Marie Jackson-Randolph, survived the primary. Bates and Blackmon led Blanding in the polling. Three thousand votes separated Blackmon from all of the original HOPE team. However, the HOPE team was in the run-off.

Patrick became the spokesman for the victorious HOPE team. He asserted, "We sent a message as loud as thunder and clear as a bell. The overwhelming support of the HOPE team was that our children would be the winners."[44] The general election presented an opportunity for HOPE since more voters would come to the polls.

The General Election Campaign

The incumbents hoped to win the city politicians by calling in IOUs. Their campaign relied on their personal networks to turn out supporters. Apparently the incumbents did not believe in a new school politics, as they solicited endorsements of the leading politicians. In a press conference Mayor Young and City Council President Erma Henderson endorsed incumbents Bates, Rutherford, and Blackmon. Young called the incumbents "the best we have," and charged that the HOPE team are "strangers with no record at all."[45] The Mayor added, "we'd be better off with the rascals we know than the rascals we don't know. I say let's keep these rascals."[46] The mayor went on to observe, "I don't think that the members of the board who are up for re-election are responsible for conditions; I think one of the chief problems is money and that's also on the ballot."[47]

The highlight of the campaign was a televised debate among the candidates sponsored by New Detroit, Inc., the League of Women Voters, and the Association of University Women. The League acted as moderator of the debate. Like most political debates, the much-publicized confrontation quickly became a question-and-answer period, with each candidate answering questions from the audience. The audience for the debates consisted primarily of candidate campaign staff (to applaud), leaders of the school activist community, and social welfare agency heads. There seemed to be few unaffiliated parents in the audience.

In the debate the HOPE candidates were at an advantage because they did not have to defend their records. Alonzo Bates actually attempted to defend his travel as a school board member. He cited his founding of the Bates Academy for gifted children as evidence of his leadership. Blackmon cited her experience as a reason for returning her to office. It was clear that the unpolished and confrontational style of Bates did not serve him well and confirmed the perception that he should not be returned. Blackmon's conciliatory style in the debates did not save her seat either.

The HOPE slate conducted an unrelenting attack on the judgment and the ethics of the incumbents. The candidates' campaigns consisted of making the rounds in the activist communities and the churches. In one colorful incident, two HOPE candidates rented a loaned limousine with a "NO PERKS" sign and had it towed away from the School Center Building. This dig at the use of chauffeur-driven automobiles may have accelerated the board's timetable for discontinuing the practice.

The four HOPE candidates won by more than 20,000 votes over the incumbents. HOPE won in all of the integrated neighborhoods. Marie Blackmon received the highest number of votes of the incumbents (86,784). All HOPE candidates received over 100,000 votes. Blackmon, Bates, and Rutherford, considered unbeatable in 1984, were crushed. Bates' votes came mainly from his Eastside constituency. Hayden's courting of the community organizations enabled him to be the highest vote-getter for the HOPE team. Blanding's comments were telling.

> The primary voters and the general election voters are quite different. The primary voters are a lot more informed. Those are the ones that candidates run into on campaign night; they ask a lot of questions and they usually have an idea of who they want to support. In the general election, there's a lot more name-recognition with voters involved.[48]

Detroit Federation of Teachers President John Elliot implied as much publicly. He asserted "when we have a much larger turnout in November, it may change the lists. I don't think the results repudiate the incumbents, because if it [the primary results] did, they would not have made the top eight. We still have one election to go."[49] In other words, the election is not over yet, and the union will take a wait-and-see posture. Elliott and others in the cartel had no idea the primary election would be so turbulent.

The 1988 general election, thought by many to be a watershed in school politics, did not live up to its potential. Despite generating more publicity than any Board election since 1970, the HOPE campaign did not change the pattern of voting in school politics. As was suggested, the primary voter turnout was expected to be

Figure 1 - Detroit School Board Elections, 1970-1988
(Voter turnout as % of registered voters)

Source: Detroit Board of Elections, 1988

much lower than the general election. Surprisingly, the primary and general elections did not represent a record turnout of voters. The 1988 Democratic presidential campaign in Michigan did not increase voter turnout as it had in 1980. Figure 1 shows the voting patterns discussed in this paper.

Figure 1 also shows that the HOPE team campaign did not generate a record turnout. The primary results did not match the primary election of 1982, an election to recentralize the school board primarily promoted by the school cartel. The lowest voter turnout was in the 1984 primary. If this was a critical election for the school cartel, there should have been a higher turnout. The results suggest that the threat from the insurgent HOPE team was viewed as insurmountable. The more intriguing aspect of the turnout was that most registered voters continued their habit of not voting in school elections.

However, there was a danger in inviting so many voters into school politics. It is clear that some HOPE voters went to the polls because they were embarrassed by the scandal. The indignant voter is not uncommon in school elections. Alonzo Bates attributes his defeat to the media. He opined "I am an activist. I am clean. I don't drink, do drugs. Why wouldn't they support (them) HOPE team? They (media) wanted someone they could control."[50] He denied that he was the mayor's representative on the board.

Frederick Wirt found that occasionally school politics contain extremely disturbing issues. He asserted, "these turbulent issues turn the usual dry arroyos of school electoral channels into a flash flood, with the careers of authorities strewn all over the bank after it passes, if they are not sufficiently resilient."[51] Chauffeured cars, expensive travel practices, and the deficit proved to be the unsettling issues for Detroiters. These were such hot issues that the legitimacy of the school cartel and school performance were rarely mentioned. The election was carefully fought over personalities and peccadilloes.

Any time a veteran of the school cartel is replaced, there is a period of adjustment. The immediate response of sitting board members came in an attempt by the lame duck board members to elect the Rev. Jim Holley, an activist preacher, outspoken supporter of Jesse Jackson, and a critic of HOPE, to serve out George Bell's remaining term. Holley was promoted as the grass-roots candidate but was seen by the HOPE supporters as a defender of the status quo. On election night, over 100 school activists showed up to vote. The incoming HOPE team supported Josh Mack, a former board member. Agreement on election procedures required twenty-one roll call votes. A *Detroit Free Press* editorial called the affair a circus. It declared "the latest series of public meetings by a lame duck body have led to such an unbelievable display of incompetence, cynicism, petty scheming, clashing egos, and erratic personal behavior that the spectacle would make the Marx Brothers look statesmanlike."[52] The paper spoke too soon. The real circus was yet to come.

Millages and Millions

The other issues on the ballot were a proposal for millage renewal and one for millage increase. The district had been haunted by a continuous fiscal crisis. The district's budget for the 1988 fiscal year was $801 million. Of this amount, $660 million was to be spent on salaries and benefits. Despite the amount spent on salaries, Detroit teachers made less than their suburban counterparts. A deficit of $160 million was unparalleled in the history of Detroit schools. If the district had any chance of solving its deficit problems, it needed a millage increase. The board hadn't lost a millage election since 1980. In 1985 the board was successful in securing a 2.25 mill increase. The 1985 victory was accomplished with a 33.9% turnout of voters.

The school activists (particularly the HOPE team) endorsed the millage renewal but were lukewarm about the increase. The HOPE campaign threatened to bring in more dissatisfied voters, so everyone wanted to disassociate the board election from the millage. Their strategy was only partially successful, as only 42.6% of the voters participated in the election. The renewal was approved, but the increase was rejected. Peile and Hall (1973) suggested that as the turnout increases, the percentage of voters in favor of millages decreases.[53] Failure of millages occurred in

Figure 2
Detroit School Millage Elections, 1968-88
(turnout as percent of registered voters)

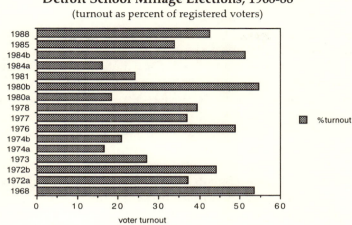

Source: Detroit Election Commission

1968, 1972, and 1976. The exception was August 1980, when there was only a 18.3% voter turnout. The board had won the November 1980 election with a 54.6 % turnout. Figure 2 shows voter turnout from 1968-88.

Coleman Young did endorse the millage election as he had done in the past. He asserted "without fail I supported the board on every millage. I had my disagreements with the board and teachers. I didn't believe that you punish the school system by cutting off the funds."[54] There was no organized opposition to the millage renewal. The millage won but the increase was rejected by voters. The failure of the 1988 millage increase gave the new board members the opportunity to restructure the appeal for a new millage election. The veteran board members insisted on a June 1989 date for a new election. The HOPE coalition wanted to delay the election. The veteran board members balked at this move, believing that off-year elections tend to bring out the school supporters. School elections conducted during a regular election tend to bring out the so-called "less informed voters." Nevertheless, HOPE felt a delay would help build credibility with the voters. The other board members finally agreed, but it took a considerable amount of HOPE team time to negotiate a delay in the vote.

In December of 1988 the special state panel delivered a devastating indictment of the District's finances. They recommended state receivership if the system did not present a deficit reduction plan and improve its fiscal management practices. The report was read by some as implying that the black managers had mismanaged school funds. Since HOPE white team member Olmstead had become chair of the finance committee, it became clear to everyone that he would be the critical player in deficit reduction negotiations with the state.

Over the Christmas holidays, there were growing efforts to force Dr. Jefferson out. Some felt that a resignation would help restore credibility to the political process and prepare the public for a new millage election. Superintendent sacrifice is a time-honored tactic of school cartels with credibility problems. Jefferson was given the option of resigning or being publicly fired. Jefferson chose the former. Jefferson agreed to fall on his sword but maintained he was ready to leave.[55]

The decision to oust Jefferson was the first test of the new board coalition of HOPE, Mack, and Everett. They agreed on Jefferson, but selecting a new superintendent would be more difficult. Apparently, the HOPE team had become convinced that the installation of a sympathetic superintendent would mean implementation of their reform program.

A New Superintendent

Four names surfaced as replacements for Jefferson. John Porter, former state superintendent and former Eastern Michigan University President, was the choice of the Hope Team. The selection of Porter was a done deal until the community activists disrupted the meeting, objecting to the Porter appointment as interim superintendent. Porter had offered to work on an on-loan basis as acting superintendent for $1. The meeting became circus-like with shouting and people being forcibly ejected from the room. Activists demanded a city resident who would hire deputies from the existing staff.

The Porter proposal was denounced by the veteran board members as a power play by the HOPE team. They offered as a compromise candidate Arthur Carter, a county supervisor. The entire deal to recruit Porter became undone. Former board president Cobbin announced publicly that Porter was unacceptable to the old board members. She and her colleagues were prepared to teach the HOPE Team a lesson in the politics of selecting staff. The HOPE team had not anticipated the resources available to their opponents and the difficulty of assuaging fears of the community. The fight over Porter's appointment consumed a tremendous amount of energy and was a lesson for the HOPE coalition.

The HOPE team strategy at board meetings became sidetracked by procedural entanglements. HOPE team members had to concede the procedural points of their opponent and adhere to board traditions. Kerr suggests that new board members, regardless of political views or mandate, could not survive the socialization process without internalizing old board views. Kerr claims that old board members will use "condescension, paternalism, chiding and even humiliation" to keep freshman members in line.[56] Veteran board members resisted most, if not all, of the initial proposals offered by the HOPE team. Although HOPE had a majority on some issues, they had to negotiate with the minority.

After considerable negotiation, the HOPE team was able to resurrect the Porter nomination. The HOPE team was able to elect Dr. Porter superintendent (6-4). None of the old members voted for Dr. Porter. Porter had to accept the appointment of Arthur Carter as deputy at the same salary as his other appointed deputies. Almost immediately after taking office, Porter began announcing cuts for the current school year. These included layoffs, school closings, termination of extracurricular activities and bus service. He promised to restore these cuts if the millage was approved.

Porter had a mandate to improve the district's financial image. He never intended to become permanent superintendent. In July 1991 the school hired Dr. Deborah McGriff, a deputy superintendent in Milwaukee. She was the first female superintendent and had worked in the reform movement in Milwaukee. Now that the HOPE had its superintendent, expectations of reform were very high. Dr. McGriff was not in office a year before she began receiving resistance to the school-based management idea. In the fall of 1992 the Detroit Federation of Teachers (DFT) went out on strike. The school empowerment plan was one of the issues. The DFT claimed that school-based management undermined the union contract and personnel rules. However the real agenda was an all-out mobilization against the HOPE team. A new cartel strategy emerged. They would claim that site-based management schools, compact schools, and other specialized schools were being funded at the expense of neighborhood schools. Although researcher Marion Orr and his associates saw the mounting opposition as community generated, they came to a similar conclusion.

> Reforms began to be cast as elitist, and that perception resonated in many Detroit communities. Out of this opposition movement emerged a group of candidates that sought to depose the HOPE team incumbents. The challengers were not running on a single slate, but generally agreed that neighborhood schools had been neglected by the board and Superintendent McGriff and that too much emphasis had been placed on the minority of students who were college-bound.[57]

The 1992 election saw the HOPE team members Blanding, Hayden, and Olmstead lose their seats. The cartel won after painting HOPE as anti-union and elitist. Even Mayor Young was convinced HOPE and Dr. McGriff were elitists.[58] McGriff's problem grew worse with the defeat of HOPE key members, and she was forced to resign in October of 1993. Thus with the demise of HOPE went the hope for school reform.

Summary

Reform and reformers do not fare well in Detroit's school politics. Mirel compares the liberal-labor-black reformers to their more elite predecessors in Detroit's golden years in the 1920s. He claims that the 1960 version of the reformers collapsed when they achieved most of their goals—integrating the system's teachers and administrators, curriculum reform, and strengthening the teachers union.[59] Despite these so-called achievements, the reform leaders were recalled.

In 1970 the formation of recall groups indicated the widespread dissatisfaction over the desegregation plans. Rossell, in her analysis of three cities with similar recall elections, correctly pointed out that the recall of Detroit board members took place before the plan was actually implemented. Although Detroit had a low voter turnout (35.1%) compared to the two other cities, Detroit had the highest level of dissent to cartel affiliated candidates (51.6%). She concluded that "electoral dissent as defeat of incumbents is probably a better measure of conflict than either turnout or the closeness of elections"[60] Desegregation of Detroit schools was a failure because white parents and citizens lacked confidence in the school board and the general quality of Detroit's schools. This is not to gainsay that racism was not a factor, but white parents felt their interests were not being represented. They saw integration and busing as yet another indication of declining quality. When it became clear that integration was inevitable, whites simply left the school system.

The school cartel responded by socializing new black members. The tenure of the liberal-labor-black coalition forced it to further incorporate the union leaders into the cartel, but the incorporation did not change existing administrative or educational policy. Indeed, it was the black administrators and union that facilitated the recentralization of the school system. With the union covered the cartel seemed stronger than before.

Apparently the 1987 scandal was not disruptive enough to fundamentally change the array of power within the cartel. However, the short term fallout from the 1988 campaign reveals how the cartel acted to insulate itself from outsiders. The whispered theme of the incumbents in the 1988 election was that "whites are attempting to embarrass 'us.'" Black voters were told to thwart this effort to embarrass the race. This tactic did not work, as the chauffeured car incident eliminated any possibility of its success. The cartel interest was served by sacrificing a few board members while retaining some policy control. HOPE team members ran into the institutional barriers to their reform. They could not reshape the agenda of the school board. Goldhammer observed "the school board was to a large extent self-perpetuating, but its capacity to perpetuate itself was contingent upon the ability of the power structure to sustain its supremacy in the face of challenge."[61]

The hand of the power structure could be seen in the funding and staffing of the HOPE campaign. The County Executive's staff assisted the HOPE slate. The economic elite, exemplified by the Chamber of Commerce, supported HOPE in 1988, but it threatened to withdraw support from the system if the HOPE defeat did not deter voters from voting the HOPE team out. Marion Orr and associates saw the failure of HOPE "as a story of personal leadership."[62] Critics of the HOPE team found them to be "clumsy and heavy handed."[63] The researchers also laid some of the blame on Dr. McGriff's administrative style and personality. Not only did she not become a "Detroiter," she refused to sell her foreign car.[64] She also managed to alienate board members, particularly the president, April Howard Coleman.

An alternative explanation was that the cartel had recovered from the 1988 elections. In forcing the HOPE team to spend so much time and resources recruiting a replacement for Dr. Jefferson and mobilizing for a millage increase, the cartel was able to capitalize on the mistakes of the reformers. The HOPE team did not build an electoral constituency. The support they received from the white dominated Chamber of Commerce served to undermine their credibility in the city's black community. Some members of the black community shared a view that HOPE was a white-backed plot to take over the schools. Former Mayor Coleman Young shared this view.

> HOPE was sponsored politically by McNamara (Wayne County Executive). I don't know if he fully understood their intent. He wanted to get political hegemony through the school board. It had been his ambition to control Detroit and then have certain control over the state.[65]

The former mayor added:

> I was not sympathetic toward the HOPE team. HOPE came in with some ideas. It was some form of parochialism. They talked about empowerment but it was a new concept from conservative circles. They talked about competition and individual charter schools. They say, let us privatize schools. They were not in control long enough to do anything.[66]

Finally, the 1992 election offered an interesting twist. Larry Patrick, the Republican member of the HOPE team was the only one that survived the election. A new superintendent was recruited from inside candidates, and the cartel returned to business as usual.

NOTES

1. See David Katzman, *Before the Ghetto: Black Detroit in the Nineteenth Century* (Urbana: University of Illinois, 1973).

2. See Jeffrey Mirel, *The Rise and Fall of an Urban School System: Detroit, 1907-1981* (Ann Arbor: The University of Michigan Press, 1993).

3. Ibid.

4. See Barry Bluestone and Benjamin Harrision, *The Deindustrialization of America* (New York: Basic Books, 1989).

5. See *Report of the Citizens Advisory Committee on School Needs* (Detroit: Detroit Board of Education, 1958).

6. *The Finding and Recommendation of the Citizens Advisory Committee on Equal Education Opportunity* (Detroit: Detroit Board of Education, 1962).

7. Mirel, p. 274.

8. Ibid., p. 298.

9. Mirel, p. 299.

10. Marvin Pilo, "A Tale of Two Cities: The Application of Models of School Decentralization to Cases of New York City and Detroit," *Education and Urban Society* 7, No. 4 (August 1975), pp. 403-404.

11. Ibid., p. 404.

12. B.J. Widick, *Detroit: City of Race and Class Violence* (Chicago: Quadrangle Books, 1972), p. 163.

13. Ibid., p. 165.

14. Ibid., p. 215.

15. See Wilbur C. Rich, *Coleman Young and Detroit Politics: From Reformer to Power Broker* (Detroit: Wayne State University Press, 1989).

16. William R. Grant," Community Control vs. School Integration-The Case of Detroit," *The Public Interest* , No. 24, (Summer 1971), p. 63.

17. Mirel, op. cit.

18. Grant, op. cit. 73.

19. C.T. Clotfelter, "Detroit Decision and White Flight," *Journal of Urban Law* 5 (January 1976): 99-112.

20. *Milliken v. Bradley*, op. cit.

21. This conclusion was made after an interview with Superintendent Arthur Jefferson. He was a regional superintendent before he became General Superintendent, April 17 1994.

22. Rich, op. cit.

23. Jeffrey Hadden, "Young Urges New Method of Public Financing," *Detriot News* (December 1977), p. 1b.

24. Rich, op. cit.

25. Hadden, op. cit.

26. Ibid.

27. Interview with Arthur Jefferson, April 17, 1990.

28. Interview with Coleman Young, September 8, 1994.

29. C. Cain and R. Russell, "No Loan If Driver Stays," *Detroit News* (May 11, 1988), p. 1.

30. Ibid.

31. Ibid.

32. Lutz and Wang, 1988, p. 67.

33. Interview with a former board member, 1989.

34. Interview with Coleman Young, op. cit.

35. Cassandra Spratling, "New Detroit's Chief Assail Schools," *Detroit Free Press* (May 6, 1988), p. 1.

36. Russell,

37. Cassandra Spratling, op. cit.

38. Cassandra Sprating, May 6, 1988, op. cit., p. 1.

39. Interview with Horace Sheffield, August 1989.

40. HOPE Team handout.

41. Interview with Ed Simpkin, August 7, 1989.

42. Cain and Russell, 1988, p. 1A.

43. Jeffrey Finkleman, "Bell, Bates Rank a Top City School Travel List," *Detroit Free Press*, (May 23, 1986), p. 1.

44. Darryl Fears and L. Carol Richie, "School Vote Call a Jolt," *Detroit Free Press* (May 23, 1988), p. 1.

45. Brenda Gilchrist, "School Race Incumbents Get Backing," *Detroit Free Press* (October 19, 1988), p. 1.

46. Ibid.

47. Ibid.

48. Fears and Richie, p. 8A.

49. Ibid., p. 1.

50. Interview with Alonzo Bates, August 3, 1989.

51. Frederick Wirt, ed., *The Polity of the Schools* (Lexington, MA: Lexington Books, 1975), p. 4.

52. Editorial, "School Board: It 's Time to End the Circus Act and Wait for New Members," *Detroit Free Press* (December 1, 1988), 8A.

53. Phillip Peile and John Stuart Hall, *Budgets, Bonds and Ballots: Voting Behavior in School Financial Elections* (Lexington: D.C. Heath, 1973).

54. Interview with Coleman Young, September 8, 1994.

55. Interview with Arthur Jefferson, 1994.

56. N.D. Kerr, "The School Board As An Agency of Legitimation," *Sociology of Education*, 38 (1964), p. 46.

57. Marion Orr, Richard Hula, Fernando Guerra and Mara Cohen "Sources of Educational Reform: Changing Actors in Shifting Arenas," paper presented at Midwest Political Science Association, Chicago, 1995, p. 12.

58. Interview with Coleman Young, 1994.

59. Mirel, p. 404.

60. Rossell, p. 61.

61. Keith Goldhammer, "Community Power Structure and School Board Membership," *The American School Board Journal* , 130 (March 1955): 23-25.

62. Orr et al., p. 15.

63. Ibid.

64. Ibid., p. 16.

65. Interview with Coleman Young, 1994.

66. Ibid.

CHAPTER 3

Gary School Politics

Gary, Indiana, located in the shadow of Chicago, is the epitome of a rust-belt mill town. Gary is the little city that U.S. Steel made, occupying 10 miles along the south shore of Lake Michigan. Howard Peckham, in his bicentennial history, observed "though Gary is Indiana's third largest city in size, it is the least Hoosier in character and not a center for any area."[1] Edward Greer (1979), in his book *Big Steel*, called Gary "a microcosm of heartland industrial America."[2] The history of Gary schools parallels the establishment of the town in 1906. The town was named after Elbert Gary, the leader of U.S. Steel, who selected this area just across the Illinois line. The Gary Works of U.S. Steel Corporation drew people from across the nation. Rumors of good jobs in the foundry drew workers from the big cities to the West. Gary was more than a mini-Pittsburgh. With its billowing smokestacks, it represented rural Indiana's claims to being on the nation's industrial team.

As one would expect, the history of Gary school politics interweaves with its iron and steel base. U.S. Steel was responsible for the location of the city, planning its streets and development of its schools. Since Gary Works represented the state of the art technology in 1906, the steel companies were interested in developing an innovative school system to produce workers who could produce good steel. This chapter reviews the evolution of Gary schools and their separation from the economy.

Gary, a Cradle of Reform?

No one questioned that Gary schools were expected to provide education for steel workers. William A. Wirt was brought to Gary from Bluffton, Indiana, to organize the first school system in Gary.

Wirt had gained a regional reputation for creating work-study-play schools in Bluffton. Recruited by business elites to replicate this experimental school in Gary, Wirt was given total control of the system. After creating the administrative structure for the Gary schools, Wirt established the famous Gary Plan.

The Gary Plan consisted of a work-study-play system for education, and saw the school as the center of community activity. In 1912 Wirt introduced the "auditorium" components of his plan. This called for students to participate in a program of speaking and music performances. The program also allowed teachers to educate students as a group for social life and citizenship.[3] Wirt, in his foreword to Randolph Bourne's book *The Gary Schools* (1916), summarized the philosophy in two short paragraphs.

> First, all children should be busy all day long at work, study and play under right conditions.
>
> Second: Cities can finance an adequate work-study—and play program only when all the facilities of the entire community for work, study, and play of children are properly coordinated with the school, the coordinating agent, so that all facilities supplement one another and "peak-loads" are avoided by keeping all facilities of the school plant in use all of the time.[4]

The concept relied heavily on the unit system, under which all grades were together in the same building. The emphasis was on cultural development and family relationships in schools. The older children were expected to look after their younger siblings. The work-study plan was very popular because it met the needs of the steel industry in teaching the European immigrants (Lithuanians, Slovenes, Greeks, and Poles) English while training them for work in the mills.

Wirt's tenure lasted from 1907-1938. An active anti-Communist, Wirt once wrote he had evidence that there was a plot to change the American economy. These views endeared him to his mentors in the steel industry. Respected by the steel elite, Wirt was given the resources to build a school system that was "tightly coupled" with the growing steel industry. During Wirt's era Gary gained the reputation of one of the most progressive school systems in the nation. Educators from all over the nation converged on Gary to observe his methods. The *Post Tribune* of Gary opined, "The reason is that Gary schools are the most advertised educational institutions in the world today. They have been justly termed the educational wonder of America."[5]

Wirt's impact on Gary schools cannot be underestimated. He was described by one of his former employees as a "benevolent dictator" who managed the board as well as the school system. Wirt was an educational giant in his time, but there is little evidence that he gave a lot of thought to improving the education of black children. In 1910 there were 383 blacks among the city's population of 16,802. Blacks started to flock to Gary from the South to work in the mills as the nation entered World War I. By 1920 their numbers had grown to 5,299 out of a total of 55, 378 residents or about 10%.

At first blacks were integrated into the general population. As their numbers grew, white parents and students objected to attending the same schools. Wirt declared, "We believe that it is only in justice to the Negro children that they be segregated."[6] Wirt began establishing black elementary schools and recruiting black teachers. William Gleason, U.S. Steel superintendent, advocated segregated housing for blacks. Accordingly, blacks were carefully segregated in separate schools as they aggregated into contained housing patterns. Blacks were increasingly forced to live in the central district.

The Making of Black Schools

Haron J. Battle became one of the first black school administrators, first as supervisor of secondary schools in 1956 and as assistant superintendent in 1965. He cited 1927 as a critical turning point in the history of blacks in Gary schools. Blacks struck against the Virginia Street School, claiming discrimination and overcrowding in the black schools. The board did transfer some black students from the overcrowded school to Emerson School. White students struck against integration. This dilemma led the mayor and City Council to appropriate the money for an annex to the Roosevelt High School for Negroes, but they ignored further pleas for school desegregation. According to Battle, the thirties was an interesting period for black students in Gary schools. The New Deal also had a profound impact upon Gary schools.

Still a segregated minority, black students of that era were privileged to hear some of the nation's most distinguished black leaders. The district brought in famous black scholars and celebrities to lecture and to make appearances in the schools. The list included Dr. W.E.B. DuBois, James Weldon Johnson, Mary McCloud Bethune, Paul Robeson, Mordecia Johnson, and Joe Louis. Yet the schools remain segregated, as Gary housing patterns reflected the rigid separation of the races.

Established in 1925, Roosevelt High would eventually become a predominately black school. Blacks began attending Roosevelt in the twenties. Two years later, school officials built a separate building for blacks. The hiring of E.D. Simpson, the school's first black teacher, was considered a major breakthrough. In 1927 Wirt brought H. Theodore Tatum, from the New Orleans school system to be the first black principal of Virginia Street School. He found blacks segregated in terrible facilities. "It looked like a line of shanties. I told him, 'I won't stay more than two years unless you find another place.'"[7] Tatum never left, though, and became the first black principal of Roosevelt High School. In this capacity Tatum lamented Gary's job ceilings for blacks. He observed, "Black boys who had academic ability would not go into the mill. There was no chance for advancement then, and now they are lost to Gary."[8] Gary exported its best and brightest elsewhere.

Yet black educators were able to enjoy some social mobility. Warren M. Anderson, one of Roosevelt's teachers, was the first black to serve on the state Board of Education. Roosevelt became the institutional mentor for many prominent black Garyites. In the 1940s Bishop Claude Allen became the first black appointed to Gary school board. As of 1950, however, most blacks were still forced to go to a single high school, Roosevelt.

Froebel, one of the schools Wirt built, became the city's only integrated school. It boasted about being the first high school in Indiana to take an integrated basketball team to the state tournament. High school basketball is a passion in Indiana. Nevertheless, Froebel had a terrible reputation for mistreating black students. Blacks were denied opportunities to participate in all other extracurricular activities and were allowed to use the swimming pool but once a week. Black members of the basketball team were not invited to participate in victory rallies. In response to the 1943 Detroit riot and resultant unrest in Gary, the board hired a New York City firm, Intercultural Education, to redesign its curriculum. Initial efforts failed.

In 1945 white students protested attending schools with blacks. In 1946 the board passed a resolution affirming the principle of the geographic attendance area. For the first time in Gary's history, blacks were not forced to go to all-black elementary and secondary schools. The process started at the middle school level, and one by one, the grades were integrated. In the same year blacks organized the second major boycott of the schools. The strikes ended only when the board promised to end all segregated schools. In 1947 the board promulgated a desegregation policy for the district. Nevertheless, few black children attended integrated schools because they did not live in integrated attendance zones. The state of Indiana outlawed de jure segregated schools in 1949. De facto segregation became the primary way to separate the races. The resentment that built up over the fifties would explode when these graduates became adults.

Gary schools continued to use Wirt's curriculum ideas long after his tenure, mainly because his successors were administrators, not curricular innovators. For the next thirty years Gary superintendents would consider themselves administrators. During this period Gary saw a series of superintendents but none with the political clout and national visibility of William Wirt. McKinney concluded that "despite personal coldness and brusqueness, Wirt had garnered a large and devoted group of people around him and his schools."[9] Wirt had "built a system that was responsive only to him."[10]

During WWII the city underwent a period of incredible growth, particularly among the black population. Blacks settled mainly in the black neighborhoods. Froebel High School became almost completely black. Yet no one formally challenged the de facto segregation in the 1950s. Even after *Brown v. Board of Education,* the district made no effort to desegregate the school system. In June of 1954 the district commissioned a major study of the school system by the Public Administration Service. Despite the fact that this study was commissioned a month after the famous desegregation case, the 1955 report made no mention of the de facto segregation in Gary's schools. The report did allow that the Gary community, particularly the business community, had lost confidence in the Gary schools. Whatever worker readiness image that had been created by the Wirt era no longer existed. The report concluded that "virtually" all Gary industrial and business establishments hired "off-the-street." That is, they did not recognize the school system as a source of well-prepared employee prospects and did not turn to graduating classes in an effort to find promising employee candidates.[11]

By the middle of the decade the enrollment of Gary's schools had reached its peak. There were over 48,000 students and the population was growing. Superintendent Arnold Blankenship took the responsibility of dismantling most of the Wirt legacy, particularly the unit system. He introduced the concept of the middle school and built separate elementary schools. The high school became grades 8-12. Blankenship also separated the vocational schools. In 1956 he appointed Dr. Battle, a black man, as supervisor of secondary schools. There was little objection to reforms because of the "white flight."[12] The remaining whites were protected by the neighborhood concept. Yet black politics of access and recognition continued as the goal of hiring more black teachers and ending de facto segregation had not been reached.

Courts and De Facto Segregation

By 1960 the black population constituted 39% of Gary residents, and they began to agitate for political incorporation. Politicized by the civil rights movement in the South, a new generation of black professionals sought incorporation into Gary school politics as such; they began to protest the mistreatment of black children in Emerson Elementary School and to demand more black teachers. In June of 1962 a group of blacks, led by Jesse Bell, Jr. and represented by Richard Hatcher, a young lawyer, filed a discrimination suit against the school board claiming that it deliberately fostered a de facto system. They argued that attendant zones were arbitrary, and thus the boundary lines were arbitrarily designed to maintain the segregation of the races. The black plaintiff hired Dr. Max Wolff, an expert on de facto segregation, to make their case before the court. The plaintiffs in *Bell v. Schools, City of Gary* amassed an incredible amounts of data supporting their claims.[13] They cited housing patterns, teacher recruitment, and school records, but they still lost the case. After reviewing the case, John Kaplan found that the two sides, both blacks and whites, had different views about integration.[14]

Most blacks were convinced that the quality of education, both in physical facilities and teaching, was better in the white schools. They believed that all black schools were potentially psychologically damaging to their children. However, most whites did not want their children to go to school with blacks. This sentiment was based, in part, on the belief that the great majority of blacks were of lower-class origin and were not fit to be companions or schoolmates for their children. These whites asserted that although they had no objections to their children attending schools with middle-class black children, the education and development of their children would be affected by contact with lower-class blacks. Others, perhaps more numerous in Gary and concentrated in lower-class white areas, took a different view. They frankly did not want integrated schools.

In January of 1964, there was a confrontation between Mayor Martin Katz and the president of the school board. Andrew White, a leader of the steel union, led a fight to fire Superintendent A.H. Blankenship. Blankenship had alienated board members by not supporting the board in its fight with the North Central Accreditation Association and the teacher strike of that year. Mayor Katz became publicly involved in the dispute between the superintendent and the board. White accused Katz of political interference. The Mayor reacted by issuing the following statement.

"The charge of political interference by the Mayor obviously lacks foundation in truth, because if it were possible for the mayor to interfere effectively, the present school board would be replaced without further delay. . . . It is a good policy of the law for the Mayor not to be able to interfere with the operation of the school board. But it is neither the intent nor the policy of the law for the school board to be able to isolate itself from the needs and desires of the community."[15]

Although this dispute had little to do with de facto segregation, the black community supported Mayor Katz. They, along with the PTA, organized a gigantic petition drive of over 22,000 signatures to replace the board. The drive was led by Rev. John Hunter and Jack Burns of the PTA and Citizens' Committee, respectively. The Katz/White controversy served to politicize the black communities around educational issues.[16] Katz had appointed blacks to the board and to other city commissions, and blacks held important positions in his administration. The dispute between White and Katz awakened the public to the intensity of black discontentment with the school system.

In April of 1964 the Civil Rights Coordinating Committee (CRCC), led by Jeanette Strong, sponsored a Freedom Day boycott to protest against de facto segregation. They claimed, consistent with the logic of *Brown v. Board of Education* (1954), that separate schools were psychologically damaging to black students. They reasoned that the way to change the system was to withdraw black participation from de facto segregated schools. They set up so-called Freedom Schools around the city to accommodate black students. They taught race pride and reviewed the activities of the ongoing southern Civil Rights Movement. Although resisted by the board, the boycott facilitated the transfer of some black students to the Horace Mann School, a previously all-white school. This was the first successful post-*Brown* protest of school policy by black citizens and the beginning of a new tradition of citizen-based groups in school politics.

In 1967 the Gary Human Rights Commission issued a report which further exposed the de facto segregated system still operating in the city. The report, written by Harriet Gross, recommended eight points to improve and integrate the schools. These included: establishment of a formal policy on integration, establishment of a Citizen's Advisory Committee on School Integration, location of future school sites to maximize school integration, establishment of a community education program on the disadvantages of social and racial isolation, assistance of teachers in an integrated setting application for federal funds for program implementation, publication of school achievement scores to show the disabling effects of racial imbalance in schools and the regular publication of data on racial imbalance. This report was a beginning of the confrontation between the commission and the school board. Thus Gary's blacks entered the second stage of involvement in school policy, the politics of competition and confrontation.

Cohen observed that "the Gary schools had survived over fifty years of growth and development, storm and strife, years of fortune and years of famine. Once in the forefront of educational change, they entered the 1960s huddled in the middle of the institutional pack along with most city school systems."[17] The summer of 1967 was a long hot summer for most of urban America. There were major riots in Detroit and Newark. Blacks in Gary were equally discontented, but they directed their energies into political organizing. Younger black professionals were able to seize control of the grass-roots sentiment and convert it into a political movement. The discontentment over schools, along with other racial issues gave rise to the emergence of a young lawyer named Richard Hatcher.

The Election of Richard Hatcher

Richard Hatcher represented the perfect example of a Horatio Alger story in American politics. Born in 1933 to a poor family of thirteen children in Michigan City, Indiana, he overcame adversity to become a major urban politician. A product of the public school system, Hatcher became one of the city's most prominent black lawyers. In 1960 Hatcher co-founded an independent black political group called Muiguithania, led by black professionals.

Muiguithania eventually became a Democrat reform club. The Democratic Party in Gary, dominated by the Lake County Democratic Organization, had a reputation of being a political machine and tolerating corruption. Although Hatcher began his career in the party as a lawyer in the county prosecutor's office, a traditional entry-level job for would-be politicians in the Lake County Organization, he was able to campaign as a reformer.

It was his role as one of the principal lawyers in a 1962 desegregation suit against Gary schools that created Hatcher's civil rights mystique. In 1963 he ran for City Council with the support of Muiguithania and won. He quickly became the most visible black politician in the county and in the state. After five years in City Council he ran for mayor. Hatcher's election has been the subject of several analyses mainly because it represented one of the first victories of a black politician in an industrial Northern city. Scholars Alex Poinsett,[18] William Nelson,[19] Edmond Keller,[20] Roger Oden[21] and Ed Greer[22] have painstakingly analyzed the mechanisms of this unexpected 1967 victory. They all agree that black voters (93% of the black voters voted for Hatcher) were primarily responsible for Hatcher's primary victory. Scholars found Gary fascinating because Hatcher's efforts were aimed at reforming Democratic politics with what they considered a black nationalist ideology.

More importantly, Hatcher's school policy campaign issues were submerged under the general enthusiasm and historical significance of his campaign. Hatcher was so popular that most of the city's black residents were working to get him elected. His army of volunteers included some teachers and administrators. Lee Gilbert, the superintendent of schools, complained that Hatcher supporters were campaigning in the schools. Gilbert issued a memo which forbade campaigning on school property. However, teachers could wear buttons or permit students to conduct straw votes on the election.

Teachers, particularly the black ones, supported Hatcher's promotion of integrated schools. Hatcher also attacked the board for keeping certain black schools near black neighborhoods. Hatcher recalled, "Blacks were confined to the central district. If a new school was built, it was built on the fringes of the black community. The ghetto would expand to that school. There was no integration. There was overcrowding in schools in Midtown. The outlying schools in Glen Park, Miller, and the Far Westside had empty seats. It was an attempt to contain the black community."[23] Other school-related issues were board membership of a single token black member of the board in a system with predominately black student body, lack of black administrators (principals) and athletic directors.

After Hatcher was elected, he instantly became a national black spokesperson for inner-city problems. While Gary and Hatcher were getting media attention, there was a growing undercurrent over the continuing segregation of Gary schools. The political pressure of change in the schools came primarily from black nationalists and other radical groups, which advocated more control over schools by blacks. Hatcher was committed to change the status quo, but first he had to make school board appointments on the board. The pressure grew so intense that the school cartel had to do something. Superintendent Gilbert was replaced by acting superintendent Clarence Swingley.

Hatcher and School Politics

In 1968 the Concerned Citizens for Quality Education (CCQE), a small loosely-organized group of political activists and parents, were searching for a way to protest the segregation policies of acting Superintendent Clarence Swingley. The acting superintendent's tenure started with a very inexpedient incident. He had a public altercation with a Mexican-American woman at Edison Elementary School and managed to alienate the Hispanic community. Hispanics joined blacks as critics of Swingley's administration.

CCQE claimed that black children, the majority student population, were not receiving fair treatment in schools. The Indiana Human Relations Commission supported the group's complaints that since the system was mainly black (83%), more integration was needed. Steve Morris, a former PTA president at

Frederick Douglass Elementary, reports that it was easy to organize people around something negative. His first tactic was to enlist the help of the school dropouts and have them apply peer pressure. He told the dropouts that "the reason that they could not read was (because of) the school system and the racism there."[24] He then solicited the school children to join his campaign. "We also knew that Gary was a Union town. We had pickets at schools at all times. We knew the parents would not cross the picket line."[25]

Morris also claims to have told the mayor of the planned actions. The Concerned Citizens for Quality Education held a week-long boycott of schools to protest the continuing segregation policies of schools under acting superintendent Swingley. This was followed by a school boycott , which lasted for several days and included 20,000 students. Initially Hatcher tried to remain neutral and claimed that he was concerned only as a private citizen. Morris, as spokesperson for CCQE, led a small group of adults in a takeover of the administration building. Morris gives credit to the idea of building takeover to Bernice Terry. The group took over the switchboard and informed all callers that the building was temporarily closed. This tactic proved to be a turning point for the boycott. The mayor had to abandon his neutral position and negotiate with the boycotters. A group of whites from the Glen Park Community threatened to march on City Hall. "We said we were going to intercept them."[26]

An additional group of white citizens calling themselves "Citizens to Save Our Schools" also announced that they wanted an audience with the mayor. Poinsett reported that the mayor had received reports of a potentially violent confrontation between the groups. This presented a very delicate situation for the new mayor and threatened his relationship with his basic constituency. Hatcher abandoned his publicly neutral position and proceeded to act as a mediator. He explained, "What we were going to have on our hands could have well been a bloody mess. It was at that point that I felt both a physical kind of fight and the well being of the city was in jeopardy."[27] Hatcher intervened with Steve Morris and the boycott was called off. The boycott leaders met with the board and agreed on an integration plan and the dismissal of

Swingley. Everyone was able to save face and the new mayor looked like a crisis manager.

During this period, community control became the new issue of the black civil rights movement in the North. Bernice Terry, a CCQE official, suggested that black schools be separated from white supervision. She wanted division of the finances and separate schools so that blacks could name their own schools, boards, and superintendents. She reported that the Gary schools were 62% black. "It is ridiculous to go up before a Board with one Negro member. . . . We shall proceed to get our own school board and it will be a body of people committed to the highest ideas of Democracy and to a program designed to make these ideas work."[28]

The community control movement never took hold in Gary. The reasons may be traced back to political styles of the city. Gary in many ways is an example of V.O. Key, Jr.'s notion of friends and neighbors politics, i.e., small town environments breed a special kind of personalized politics. Everyone seems to know everyone else or is related in some way to local politicians. The black community had little to gain with community control. People were convinced that the black mayor could eventually change the composition of the board and accomplish all of the goals of community control. However, the mayor's role in school policy was restricted by law. He could appoint the school board, but the board appointed the superintendent. The law also required that a member of the opposite party be represented on the board. Hatcher's predecessor, Martin Katz, created the Mayor's Commission on School Board Appointments. Hatcher continued the procedure. Under Katz it was a thirty-five member committee which reviewed the credentials of prospective board members. Hatcher asked his committee to narrow the names to three, and he then selected one of the individuals for the board.

As Gary mayors had done before him, Hatcher often disavowed his influence with the board in meetings with the press. He claimed that he got involved in school matters only at the invitation of the board. This hands-off policy was different from the past when mayors would call the superintendent and tell him whom to appoint as a principal. "Board members would go into schools and tell them whom to hire."[29] Hatcher, however, was very much involved behind the scenes. Besides, his board appointments were signals to the black community about the mayor's political thinking. Hatcher's first black appointments to the board were Dr. Alfonso Holiday and Emily Caldwell. These middle-class black appointments were acceptable to the school activist community. He followed that pattern until the board had a black majority. By 1976, some appointments were considered controversial, particularly that of Maurice Preston, a political activist who was not a member of the school activist community. Some political activists suggested that the only way to get a more representative board was to switch to an elected one. Most of the Gary community opposed the idea of an elected board. Even the *Post Tribune* wrote an editorial condemning the idea. It thought that campaigning for board seats would introduce more politics into the process.

The seventies was clearly a transition period for Hatcher. The Hatcher era enjoyed six years of relative board membership stability during the eighties, more than either of the two other cities in this study. Yet he was also the first Gary mayor to be forced to deal with increasingly militant teacher unions. The American Federation of Teachers, Local #4, which was started in 1916, was recognized for collective bargaining in 1967 and had its first major strike in 1970. This strike lasted two weeks. In 1971 the union elected its first black president, Shirley Irons. Under her leadership the so-called Great Strike occurred. In 1972 the teachers began the strike on April 20 and lasted until May 22. Hatcher had to intervene as a mediator after the two sides became deadlocked. After the 1972 strike, Irons established herself and the union as major players in school politics. The union became another part of the cartel, along with the superintendents and board, that ran school affairs.

Throughout it all, Hatcher felt his relationship to the board was good. The only exception was the board's decision to close Froebel High School. "My initial reaction was that the board had a good reason to close a school, Hatcher said, that was no longer needed."[30] The Freobel alumni wanted to keep it open.

Born in Oakland, California, McAndrews was educated at the University of California, Berkeley. He was a protégé of Harold Howe, then the head of the Learning Institute of North Carolina (LINC). McAndrews succeeded Howe as director when Howe became the U.S. Commissioner of Education. Considered an expert on the learning problems of under-achieving children, forty two-year-old McAndrews was clearly a rising star in education circles. Hatcher called him "the right person for that time in city history."[35]

McAndrews told an assembly of teachers after his appointment that he was going to attack the Gary community's inferiority complex. He asserted "I didn't come here to preside over problems because places like Gary are where the action is."[36] He planned to "make Gary the best city system in the United States."[37] Given a mandate to improve the quality of Gary schools and fortified by enthusiasm, McAndrews was expansive. In his first interview with the press, he outlined two major objectives of his administration. They were: 1) To maintain the white population in Gary, to prevent an exodus from the city, so that Gary wouldn't become a Washington, D.C. He was instrumental in initiating one of the nation's first programs letting a private company operate a public school; 2) to assure "all of our parents and all of the residents of the city that there isn't a better education anywhere than they're going to able to get in Gary schools." He ended the interview with the following statement: "I'm convinced that kids in Gary are no different than the kids in North Carolina. I'm sure we'll find that the programs that worked there will work here."[38] The McAndrews administration immediately got into trouble as the new superintendent passed over the two black assistant superintendents and hired Swingley as his temporary assistant. Steve Morris immediately attacked McAndrews. He asserted "I am not implying this was done because of the Battle and Wiley's race [the men are black]. I am saying race was the reason."[39]

The McAndrews era started a flurry of proposals and administrative changes. In 1970 the board received a grant from the Rockefeller Foundation to start a community education program. McAndrews dubbed it the Reciprocal Education Program (REP). It was "designed to destroy the self-defeating walls between the helpers and the helped."[40] He wanted to establish 13 REP programs primarily in the black community. Consisting of 13 staff members of teachers and social workers, these storefront community satellite centers would create community involvement in schools and provide adult education. Parents and teachers would learn from each other.

With great drama, McAndews announced to the national educational community his intentions in Gary. "We in the Gary School System want to take education out of its tuxedo and put it in dungarees. We want to grab the three R's by their arthritic ankles and turn them upside down, and shake out the stiff-necked conventions and meaningless rote of years. We want to be part of the community, not just nervously coexist with it."[41] This program, although interesting, did not get the national education community's attention. The media attention came a year later when McAndrews led the board into contract education with a national educational research firm.

The Second Gary Plan

Behavioral Research Laboratories of Palo Alto, California, a curriculum development company, signed a $2.4 million contract to improve the reading and math scores of students at the Benjamin Banneker Elementary School. Banneker was predominantly black and enrolled 850 students. At the time Banneker sixth graders were reading at the 4.8 grade level and at the 5.1 grade level on standardized tests. McAndrews reported widespread disillusionment and dissatisfaction among Banneker parents. The contract called for improvement at the end of three years or BRL would refund the city at the rate of $2,400 per student.[42]

The school board, led by Dr. Alfonso Holliday II, supported the move. He asserted, "with education costs rising 15 to 20 percent a year, we didn't feel we could keep asking for more money when our children were learning below their grade levels. We are at rock bottom and must try new approaches."[43] Otha Porter described BRL as applying a 'money-back guarantee' to education services.[44] Other educational writers were appalled at what they viewed as an unbalanced curriculum. Minnie Berson, a columnist for *Childhood Education*, reflected this sentiment.

> In a program that guarantees standardization as though children were inhuman merchandise, the compulsive push for poor-child literacy, without broad school experiential underpinnings, really seems a way of hood-winking the poverty parent who is being convinced that the program's packaged experiences— and only these—will help the child learn well at school and stay out of trouble in the community. The more rapidly we tool up for this kind of education, and the more we rejoice at its misleading measurements, the more we reject the implication that a democracy must rear all of its children by providing them with all of the resources needed to assure a stronger society through their membership....
>
> The anxious parent and the gullible press can be further convinced that the middle class must eat educational cake, but that non-middle class must live by educational bread alone because butter and jam add to the overhead and clog up the blood system.[45]

The BRL Plan became the subject of debate in the national media. Can a vendor increase the reading skills of inner city students? The issue was also heatedly debated in Gary. BRL hired 25 of the existing 34 teachers at Banneker and 28 so-called learning supervisors, mostly parents of Banneker students. The plan called for intensive tutoring and heavy involvement of parents in teaching. The latter was considered a radical step by some educators, who apparently viewed it as tantamount to challenging the credentials of teachers. This action led the Gary teacher union AFT Local #4 to oppose the new program. They were joined by the Indiana Federation of Teachers, which attacked the program as a threat to teachers. In February of 1971 the Indiana Board of Education threatened to cut off $300,000 in state aid to Banneker because of the unbalanced curriculum and use of teachers who were not certified by the State of Indiana. It actually decommissioned the Banneker school for twenty days (February 18-March 10, 1971). The school board had to ask for a waiver to continue this experiment.

The crisis over the BRL project was relieved by year-end test scores, which showed some improvement in reading and math scores. An independent evaluation found that 73 % of children had met or exceeded national levels in reading or math. The second-year results were not so encouraging. BRL failed to allay the continued opposition of the teacher union, and the program became increasingly controversial. As a result, BRL terminated the contract six months before the end of the four-year contract. Many in the Gary school community were relieved.

However, Gary's students continue to score poorly in reading and math examinations after the BRL contract was terminated. Phillip Jones, a reviewer for *The American School Board Journal*, reported a curious comment from a teacher regarding students and the contract experiment. They "quickly learned that their test performances would either benefit or hurt the contractor. Bad performances were certainly in the Banneker student's repertoire, and he may have been more anxious to make the contractor look bad than to make himself look good, especially if his favorite teacher made it clear that she didn't like the contractor."[46] The article suggested that teachers may have sabotaged the experiment to prevent a BRL success story.

Whatever the reasons for failure, Gary lost its place as a discussion topic among the nation's educational leaders. The new board members began to concentrate more on locally-based programs and local issues. The failure of BRL represented an omen for Gary school reformers, who sought ways of involving parents more in the schools and sought to incorporate a pay-for-performance scheme. The union leaders had learned to offset any attempts to replace contract teachers. They were also able to get parents out of the teaching process. It was a clear victory for the union and its members.

The Crisis over Direction

If not private vendors, then what? McAndrews responded with what he called the Basic Competence I Program. It was designed to improve the overall performance of all the students, not just those in Banneker. This program was prompted by a 1974 study which showed that graduating seniors were reading at the 8.6 grade level and had a 9.0 grade level mathematics score. Accordingly, the board adopted a minimum competency requirement for graduation. "The purpose of the policy . . . is to guarantee that all students graduate from the Gary schools competent in the basic skills, to institute preventive and remedial programs as a way of assuring this achievement, and to have all parties—staff, students, and parents—share in the responsibility for seeing that the primary goal is realized."[47] This was not a controversial program because it attempted very little that was considered new. The main concern among administrators was the escalating development costs.[48]

Meanwhile the political environment was undergoing social transformation. Blacks were demanding more representation in city government since it was now a predominately black city. In 1976 a teacher residency rule became a major part of the school policy debate. After the Philadelphia decision, many black leaders thought the board could require teachers to live in Gary. White flight, discovered in the 1970 census, was accelerating, and the city was searching for some way of lessening it. McAndrews emerged as the chief defender of the status quo. He claimed that the board did not have the power under the law to impose a residency requirement. At the time, his record showed that 26% of teachers lived outside the city. This position eroded some of McAndrew's standing in the black community.

McAndrews also found himself opposing board members on the issue of school construction and minority contractors. The board wanted minority contractors involved. However, none of the local minority contractors could get the insurance or capital to bid on the large construction project. Board members wanted the board to adopt a construction management policy which would break up the projects into smaller units and allocate them to individual contractors. McAndrews consistently opposed this idea and managed to alienate some board members.

The next crisis for McAndrews was his advocacy of the Basic Competency II Program. Initiated in 1978, it required students to select an ordinary or advanced level for high school study. Among the choices were academic studies, business studies, fine arts, practical arts, and technical studies. The program was supposedly designed to restructure the learning program so the students would acquire entry-level job skills. This new curriculum reform called for students in the eighth grade to declare vocational choices and pursue them until graduation. Some board members were incensed at the suggestion of a vocational curriculum for black students. Ruth Taylor asserted, "I cannot sit here meeting after meeting and watch the Gary schools leap backward into antebellum days of forcing students to educate their hands in this automatic age."[49] The new program was also opposed by the NAACP and the Coalition to Save Our Schools. Many of the black activists considered the vocational program racist.

Dr. McAndrews, although now considered controversial, still enjoyed the confidence of the majority of the board and the mayor. Hatcher recalled "McAndrews was a very persuasive personality. He had an exploratory attitude about education. I agreed with what he was attempting to do."[50] Hatcher agreed that McAndrews "ran into a buzz saw" with his plans. On one occasion Councilman Freeland attacked the superintendent directly in the media. Freeland asserted, "Any school system that is happy with a graduating student passing a sixth grade literacy exam is asinine; any school system that builds a $6 million swimming pool and closes three schools trying to save money in the same breath has to be grossly unintelligent."[51] Freeland called for the resignation of the superintendent. Torres, a board member, defended McAndrews and, in turn, called for Freeland's resignation. McAndrews responded, "I'm much too busy running the schools to spend time worrying about or responding to misinformed meandering."[52] Torres himself ended up resigning from the board.

By 1978 Gary school politics were in disarray. Black members of the school cartel were not able to consolidate and routinize their political power. There were several charges of conflicts of interest and nepotism among members. Members of the board, all Hatcher appointees, were fighting among themselves. The board split reached an impasse. The transition in the third stage of black involvement, consolidation of power proved to be much more difficult than members of the board anticipated. Some saw McAndrews as an obstacle to this transition.

McAndrews, the superintendent, requested a meeting with the mayor. During the meeting members John Howard and Bill McCallister offered their resignations along with a list of grievances. They claimed that the board majority had taken over administrative duties. The board was too divided to work effectively. The antics of the majority leaders of the board were an embarrassment to the school system, and they asserted that consequently school morale was suffering. They also claimed that the president made unilateral decisions without consulting the board. They concluded that the actions of the present board would hinder the search for a new superintendent and would bring in the North Central Association to investigate. The meeting was criticized by the press, but none of the participants objected to the mayor's attempt to understand what the problems were.

Eventually, black board members became increasingly dissatisfied with McAndrew's tenure and frustrated at being unable to influence his decisions. Some suggested that McAndrews' power stemmed from his close relationship with the mayor. In 1979 an effort was made to remove McAndrews, but the anti-McAndrews forces couldn't muster the vote. There was a meeting of the board with Hatcher which eased the pressure somewhat. McAndrews admitted, "I thought his [Hatcher's] role was very constructive. He deserves a lot of credit that things didn't blow up. . . . I wouldn't say he was a mediator, just a friend of the parties."[53] Clarence Currie, a leading member of the board, became disenchanted with McAndrews when he announced publicly that he did not want to stay, not even if offered a contract. Currie also believed that McAndrews had "built an infrastructure of his own and was fairly independent of the Board. Although unspoken, race was an important factor. Board members were grateful to McAndrews for positions but blacks had no control. Our [board members'] decisions were reactions to other decisions."[54]

Former Gary board member Currie and Human Relations Commission employees remember how difficult it was to convince the board to hire a black professional in a policymaking position at the school central staff. They stated:

> There were no blacks in purchasing and budgets. We saw a terrible lack of affirmative action. McAndrews would tell you that there was nobody in the pipeline. We would ask who are you training? . . . Whites would graduate from high school and could get an apprenticeship. Black high school graduates had to go on the labor deck. Management wouldn't hire blacks. The union supported the separate society. They did nothing for black workers except make speeches.[55]

Currie remembered that black engineers from Purdue University had to go out of state to get jobs. In 1928 U.S. Steel had 28,000 employees, and 60 years later there were approximately 7,000 jobs. The decline of the mills depressed the ancillary industries and businesses in the city. Currie lamented "We have not made the adjustment."[56] Yet Currie and his colleagues became convinced that one of the elements of a turnaround would be to get new leadership of the schools. Many felt it was time for black leadership in the school system.

A Black Superintendent for Gary

By 1978 McAndrews' tenure had become less secure. None of his plans were working very well and community leaders were beginning to question his judgment. Fred Hegwood, President of the NAACP, had publicly characterized McAndrews as insensitive. He asserted, "Although the Gary school superintendent is the highest paid in the state, the Gary students' overall scholastic achievement is among the poorest in the state and we're concerned."[57] Curtis Strong, NAACP member, went further. "There is no intent to infer that Dr. McAndrews is a racist, but the problems of the poor academic achievement of Gary students rested at the door of the head of the student system. The buck stops with McAndrews. His leaving is incidental. We believe he is leaving; We hope he is leaving. He never had the desire to relate to the black population."[58] McAndrews had announced he was leaving but was having second thoughts. However, his black supporters abandoned him once he had gone on record stating he was leaving. The board then voted to fire McAndrews on March 22, 1979. The firing of McAndrews was not greeted well by the public. President of the Board Preston spoke for many board members when he asserted: " School boards have fired superintendents before. It was that in this case there was an all black board firing a white superintendent."[59] Dr. Battle believes the "closing of Froebel was the triggering element in McAndrews' firing. The Mayor wanted to build housing near the school and replenish it with more students."[60] The McAndrews era, like that of Wirt, brought some national attention to Gary schools. The entire social context of Gary schools was also changing. Gary had become what McAndrews hoped it wouldn't: a predominantly black school system.

The board decided it wanted two characteristics in its next superintendent. He should be an administrator rather than a program man, and he should be black. In January of 1980 Dr. Ernest Jones, a deputy superintendent from St. Louis, became Gary's first black superintendent. When Jones arrived the district was $8 million in debt and under the state's financial supervision. Jones drew up a fiscal plan which allowed staff reduction through attrition. He also introduced a computerized budget system and new management procedures. There were two major strikes during the Jones tenure. Jones also began to have his problems with the board.

During the Jones Administration, Hatcher came under criticism from the black community regarding his choices for school board appointments. In 1984 the screening committee was having trouble recruiting a Republican member. They were looking for a replacement for Maurice Preston. Perry, chair of the committee, asserted, "We've even asked the Republican officials in the area to make recommendations. That produced no results. We know that there are some Republicans out there. We just don't know whether they are uninterested or just uninformed."[61]

Roland Lewis, a Republican, responded by calling the whole selection process a "farce. They're down there complaining about not being able to get enough applicants for the school Board vacancy when the Mayor ignores the recommendation of the committee anyway. He chooses who he wants to choose."[62] He cited several board members who had not been interviewed by the screening committee and were appointed anyway. "They say there aren't Republicans interested. That's a lie. Those Republicans just know that the process is a joke and no one in his right mind would want to go through that once they discovers what it's all about." He was particularly critical of Carol Rhodes, a white female bus driver appointed by the mayor. "Do you think the Mayor would have appointed a black person with her qualifications?"[63] Martin Yuriga, an electrician at U.S. Steel, was finally appointed by the mayor.

In December 1986 the board met and voted not to extend Jones' contract. Jones was reportedly shocked by the board's action. Irons, the President of the teacher union, supported the board's position. She stated that Jones lacked educational leadership and was hostile toward the union. According to Irons, Jones caused the union to spend money on legal fees. Clarence Currie, a board member, conceded that "Jones had moved blacks into sensitive positions in the organization but was weak on effective school programs."[64] Mayor Hatcher suggested that firing "was not in the best interest of our city or our school children. I feel Dr. Jones should have been retained. My position may not be popular with a number of people I respect."[65] Dr. Jones agreed to accept a position called special assistant to Board of Trustees, and John Stefanelli, a principal, was appointed acting superintendent.

The firing of McAndrew and Jones was testimony to the decline of Hatcher's popularity. The school cartel began to pay less attention to Hatcher's opinions about school policy. They were responding to the change in the political climate and the general decline of Gary's economy. The end of the Hatcher era was near.

The End of the Hatcher Era

Hatcher's first term was characterized by visible progress in public works. Keller notes that between 1968-1971 Hatcher constructed or upgraded 676 public housing units. He also made street improvements. These initiatives created 4,500 jobs in Gary via federal grants. Prior to 1967 there were no public housing construction projects in Gary.[66] Along with the school crisis, Hatcher's organization began to deteriorate into factions. Enough so, that the Lake County Democratic Organization ran a prominent black physician and coroner Dr. Alexander William against the mayor. "The feeling was that Hatcher had been too ideological and not pragmatic enough to make Gary work."[67] However, Hatcher easily defeated William by a 60% majority.

Hatcher's second term was marked by changing economic conditions. By 1975, unemployment had risen from 2% at the time of his first election to 12%. The steel industry responded to the strain of foreign competition with layoffs in the plant, which caused a ripple effect on all business activities in Gary. Keller found that the business establishment shrunk from 3,293 in 1973 to 3,032 in 1974. This pattern of industrial downturn continued, and other small businesses left Gary throughout the decade. Keller suggested that the "euphoric attachment black people had to the notion of Black Power appeared to have mellowed."[68] Doubts had also developed about Hatcher's overall leadership of the city.

One of Hatcher's closest allies, Dozier T. Allen, decided to challenge him in the Democratic primary. Allen claimed that he wanted to create a climate favorable to the reentry of white business. However, he lost by 57% of the vote. Again, Hatcher was given a license to lead. The decline in Hatcher victory margin represented an erosion of support among his strongest supporters in the third, fourth, and fifth districts. Black people at all levels of Gary society began to question Hatcher's leadership. The 1980s, the Reagan era, would bring difficult times for old manufacturing cities like Gary.

The Election of Thomas Barnes

After chronicling two of Hatcher's reelection campaigns, Keller concluded that "Hatcher's continued success can be attributed to two basic factors: first, his superior political organization; and second his satisfactory policy performance in the eye of the majority of the black electorate."[69] This political organization, although weakened over the years, had enough strength to beat a 1979 challenge by Hatcher's early mentor Jesse Bell, Jr. By 1981 the impact of the Reagan Administration began to be felt by most urban politicians. The federal monies that fueled the mini-turnaround in cities like Gary dried up. Yet in 1983 Hatcher defeated City Councilman Thomas J. Crump. This was the same year Reagan's National Commission on Excellence in Education released its report called *A Nation at Risk*. It warned of a "rising tide of mediocrity" and called for more rigorous standards in public schools. If the nation was about to be enveloped by this rising tide of mediocrity, then a small school system like Gary would be swept under. Hatcher's defense of two previous superintendents undermined his credibility within the education community.

In 1987 the challenge mounted by Calumet Township Assessor Thomas Barnes proved too much for the Hatcher organization. Despite Hatcher's nationwide network of contributors and supporters, he had lost too many of his basic constituencies. The abandoned homes, blighted buildings, and unemployment were evident all over the city. The twenty-year tenure had taken its toll on the mayor's reputation. The decline of the steel industry had left the city without a manufacturing base. Unemployment was touching most Gary families. Hatcher simply couldn't explain away the decline in the economy. Robert Catlin concluded "because Hatcher literally controlled every aspect of Gary's political governance, he could never point the finger at anyone else. He had exclusive power, but at the same time he found himself with absolute responsibility."[70]

Barnes was able to tag Hatcher with a failing economy. Hatcher's reputation as being anti-business community did not help his campaign. Garyites voted to give another man the opportunity to turn the city around. Catlin attributes the demise of the Hatcher regime to a hostile local press, specifically the Gary *Post Tribune*. According to Catlin the paper publishers resented the mayor's outspokenness and his charges of white racism. This was the reason the "newspaper retaliated with a never-ending barrage of bad publicity about Gary."[71]

Barnes won the election and a new era in Gary politics began. One of his first acts was to establish a task force called ACCORD. The new task force had a committee on education which attempted to outline the future of Gary's schools. The task force was directed to study the needs of the Gary schools, but little came of the group's efforts. The school activist community did not fight the attempt to establish such a group and just ignored it.

Dr. Betty Mason Arrives

In 1988 Dr. Betty Mason, a deputy superintendent from Oklahoma City recruited before Barnes was elected, became the first female and second black educator to head the Gary school system. The board had defined the problems of student performance as a lack of parent involvement. Dr. Mason's specialty was parent and community involvement in schools. She found the district in good financial shape but a board with serious political divisions. The board was divided between the so-called Hatcher appointees and the new Barnes people. She admits that Gary is not Detroit. "We have money. We are not poor. I was surprised at the money. It is the political part that is the hardest. One has to learn the political rule book. The losers fight the winners from now on. They live it [politics]. You have to be careful about who you go to lunch with. He or she may be a Hatcher man."[72]

She also discovered several programs that she felt were inappropriate. "We do too many things. The gifted and talented programs are too expensive. I resent Saturday schools for gifted students. We don't have anything outside Title 1 for struggling students."[73] These positions put Dr. Mason at odds with the political elite and school activist community whose children used these programs. The fact that school programs were more oriented towards the kids who needed them the least is a testimony to the power of the school activist community and the inversion of the school reform process.

Mason's primary goal has been to repair the relationship between the board and corporations. This strategy has not worked. Other people believe that Barnes is letting whites take over the city. "Black newspapers will say I am courting white folks. People are extremely frustrated. They have the second largest city and they can not pull it out. They (blacks) spend too much energy fighting."[74]

In 1991 Hatcher decided to challenge Barnes at a time when the census showed the city was 82.6% black, unemployment was 9.8%, and things looked even more bleak. In a *New York Times* interview, Hatcher asserted "I call them crossover politicians. In an effort to be more acceptable to the white majority, they are unwilling to address, at least publicly, those issues that are considered as black issues: poverty, racial and economic justice, housing, adequate health care. Those are fairly universal issues, but they are still afraid to address them. My question is, how dear is the price they are willing to pay?" [75] Hatcher believed that his brand of progressive politics would be preferred over Barnes' more conciliatory style. The Barnes election coalition held and Barnes was returned to office. School politics slowly came off the front page of the newspaper.

Summary

Gary schools have operated under two large shadows: William Wirt and the U.S. Steel Corporation. At first the corporation took a paternalistic view of the workers and their politics. They wanted good "workers." They were also prepared to subsidize black Republican politics. After blacks had made the switch to the Democratic party after the Depression, the new black union leaders formed a coalition with black professionals within the context of the regular Democratic party organization. Union leaders entered school politics to ensure that workers would be capable of moving into the mills. With the end of the Wirt era and the advent of militant industrial unionism, the corporation slowly backed out of the city's school policy. The teacher unions and black politics moved to fill the vacuum. After reviewing the history of Gary schools, Cohen concluded:

> More simply, I do not believe that pluralism has been
> the guiding premise of American society. Rather, it
> seem to me that Gary schools and their counterparts
> throughout the county have operated within the rather
> narrow framework of developing corporate capitalism.
> Yet, within this limited economic, political, intellectual
> and social structure there has been a general give and
> take among various and competing individuals, groups
> and organizations. And, perhaps, children have
> occasionally reaped the benefits. The Gary schools thus
> mirrored and reaffirmed the dominant ethos.[76]

The election of Hatcher was a critical turning point for the city's blacks. The year Hatcher was elected, *Business Week* declared U.S. Steel the leader of the steel industry. His populism and reliance on federal solutions created problems between his administration and the corporate steel leaders. By the 1970s the fortunes of the corporation had changed drastically. The steel industry had not fully anticipated the Japanese and European challenges to their business and had signed union contracts which prevented them from modernizing their works. Foreign competition closed most of the plants in Gary. U.S. Steel stopped hiring steel workers and began downsizing and diversified its corporation.

The election of Hatcher was a convenient time for the corporation to slowly disconnect itself from the city and school politics. The black community won the battle for political control of schools, only to see its board develop as a source of patronage for a variety of constituencies. None of the struggles had anything to do with the changing economic condition of Gary. The attempt by McAndrews to shift the school more towards the job market was soundly defeated by the professionals who now controlled the board. Hatcher, viewed as black nationalist and anti-business by some, could not reverse the deteriorating economic conditions.

Hatcher's special assistant Edward Greer, a white man, viewed the abandonment of Gary in different terms. Greer, describing himself as a disciple of Antonio Gramsci, the Italian Marxist theorist, first viewed Hatcher's election as a liberation of Gary.[77] Later he concluded that Hatcher's plans for substituting public work jobs for lost mill jobs never had a chance. He also concluded that "regardless of formal popular sovereignty, in practical terms the government does not have available policy options which would involve superseding the private economy, and political reforms which would have such an effect remain outside of the political agenda."[78] Long after Greer had this insight, Hatcher was still trying to hold onto power and create a substitute industry.

Hatcher thought that jobs created by federal grants could sustain the economy. Indeed, jobs were created during the Nixon and Carter eras. President Carter once considered Hatcher as a possible urban advisor in the White House. The election of Ronald Reagan in 1980 saw the decline of federal spending on cities. Downtown retail stores and homes were abandoned in Gary. The school policy, losing its grip in the late sixties, became completely separated from the economy from the sixties through the eighties. No discernible change has taken place in Gary's situation in the nineties.

NOTES

1. Howard Peckham, *Indiana: A Bicentennial History* (New York: W. Norton and Co., 1978), p. 8

2. Edward Greer, *Big Steel: Black Politics and Corporate Power* (New York: Monthly Review Press, 1979) p. 13.

3. H.J. Battle, *A New Look at the Auditorium Plan in the Gary Public Schools* (April 8, 1975): 1-6.

4. Randolph Bourne, *The Gary Schools* (Boston: Houghton Mifflin, 1916), pp. xvii-xviii.

5. *The Post Tribune*, (July 28, 1921), p. 1.

6. See N. Betten and R. Mohl, *Steel City: Urban and Ethnic Patterns in Gary, Indiana, 1906-1950* (New York: Holmes & Meier, 1986).

7. See Richard Elwell, "Gary Revisited," *American Education* 12 (July 1976): 16-22.

8. Ibid.

9. William L. McKinney, "The Gary, Indiana Public School Curriculum, 1940-1970," (Unpublished Ph.D., dissertation, University of Chicago, 1973), p. 207.

10. Ibid., p. 57.

11. *The Public School System of Gary, Indiana* (Chicago: Public Administration Service, 1955), p. 13.

12. Interview with Haron Battle, April 6, 1990.

13. *Bell v. Schools, City of Gary* 324 F. 2d 209.7th (1963).

14. John Kaplan, "Segregation, Litigation and the Schools, Part III: The Gary Litigation," *Northwestern University Law Review* 59, No.1 (May-June, 1964), p. 169.

15. "School Aide: Political Interference," *Post Tribune* (January 20, 1964), p. 1.

16. Leland Joachim, "22,256 'vote' for Resignation of School Board," *Post Tribune* (January 21, 1964), p. 1.

17. Ronald Cohen, *Children of the Mill* (Bloomington: Indiana University Press, 1990), p. 239.

18. See Alex Poinsett, *Black Power, Gary Style* (Chicago: Johnson Publishing Co., 1970).

19. See William Nelson, *Black Politics in Gary: Problems and Prospects* (Washington, D.C. Joint Center for Political Studies, 1972).

20. Edmond Keller, "Electoral Politics in Gary: Mayoral Performance Organization," *Urban Affairs Quarterly*, 15, No.1 (September 1979), pp. 43-64.

21. Roger Oden, "Black Political Power in Gary, Indiana: A Theoretical and Structural Analysis," (Unpublished Ph.D. dissertation, University of Chicago, 1977).

22. Greer, op. cit.

23. Interview with Richard Hatcher, August 23, 1994.
24. Interview with Steve Morris, April 10, 1990.
25. Ibid.
26. Ibid.
27. Poinsett, op. cit.
28. "CCQE Urge Racial Separation of School," *Post Tribune* (May 31, 1968), p. 1.
29. Interview with Richard Hatcher, 1994.
30. Ibid.
31. Ibid.
32. Ibid.
33. Interview with Battle, op. cit. 1989.
34. McKinney, p. 214.
35. Interview with Richard Hatcher, 1994.
36. Jim Linse, "Tells P-T of Plans for City," *Post Tribune* (July 3, 1968), p. 1A.
37. Ibid.
38. Ibid.
39. "Hiring of Swingley Race Hit," *Post Tribune* (July 5, 1968), p. 1.
40. Gordon McAndrew, "Can Institutions Change?," *Educational Leadership* 27, No. 4 (January 1970), p. 354.
41. Ibid, p. 358.
42. Gordon McAndrew, "Gary, Indiana Contracts for Operation of Entire School," *Compact*, 5 (February 1971): 10-11.
43. Ibid., p. 10.
44. Otha Porter, "Contracted School: An Instrument of Educational Change" *Journal of Negro Education* 40 (Summer, 1971):233-239.
45. Minnie Berson, "Back to Gary," *Childhood Education* 48 (October, 1971), pp. 54-55.
46. Phillip Jones, "Gary's Fling with Performance Contracting," *The American School Board Journal* 160 (February, 1973), p. 39.
47. Interview with Battle, 1979.
48. Ibid
49. H. Jackson, "Did School Chief Battle Leave Scars," *Post Tribune* (January 12 1979), p. 1.
50. Interview with Richard Hatcher, August 23, 1994.
51. Ernie Hernandez, "Councilman-School Bring Flurry of Charges," *Post Tribune* (May 18 1977), p. 1.
52. Ibid.
53. Jackson, op. cit.
54. Vernon William, "Board Member Doesn't Worry About Criticism, Says its all Lies," *Post Tribune* (February 29,1980), p. 1.
55. Interview with Clarence Currie, January 26, 1990.
56. Ibid.

57. Curtis Strong, "NAACP Officers Term McAndrews Insensitive," *Post Tribune*, June 21, 1978, p. 1.

58. Ibid.

59. William, op. cit., p. 10.

60. Interview with Haron Battle, April 1990.

61. "School Board Seat Still Open," *Post Tribune* (June 12, 1984), p. 1.

62. Ibid.

63. Ibid.

64. Interview with Clarence Currie, op. cit.

65. Michael Sangiancomo, "Supt. Jones of Vote. I Never Expected It," *Post Tribune* (December 20, 1986), p. 1b.

66. See Keller, op. cit.

67. Ibid., p. 49.

68. Ibid., p. 51.

69. Ibid., p. 49.

70. Robert Catlin, *Racial Politics and Urban Planning, Gary, Indiana, 1980-1989*. (The University Press of Kentucky, 1993), p. 200

71. Ibid.

72. Interview with Dr. Mason, August 4, 1989.

73. Ibid.

74. Ibid.

75. Bob Terry, "Hatcher Begins Battle to Regain Spotlight in Gary," *New York Times* (May 4, 1991), p. 12A.

76. Cohen, op. cit., p. xii.

77. See Greer, op. cit.

78. Ibid., p. 17.

CHAPTER 4

Newark School Politics

In 1666 Newark, New Jersey, opened its first public schools. Public schools operated for over a hundred years there before the creation of the United States of America. Over time Newark developed a separate school system for its few black children. In 1909 New Jersey officially outlawed racially segregated schools. However, the pattern of segregated housing kept the races separated in elementary grades, and the transfer rules allowed the development of predominantly black high schools. The great northern migration of blacks to New Jersey came after the Depression and accelerated during World War II. The first black member of the board of education was appointed in 1944. Despite Newark's claims of being a progressive city, black immigrants were steered into the central ward area. Blacks began arriving in large numbers in the 1950s when the city was at its population peak (440,000). The 1950 census found that 17% of the city population was black. During that period no black served in an administrative position in the school system. Black teachers didn't even gain positions on the eligibility list for administrative jobs, based on acceptable oral as well as written exams, until June of 1959. Consequently, black involvement in school politics was not as visible as it was in Detroit and Gary. By the 1960 the percentage of blacks in Newark had doubled to 36%. In 1962 the Newark Board of Education selected Verner Henry as its first black president. Whites, at least elected politicians, were trying grant blacks access and recognition on an installment plan. This strategy failed, as we shall see, as blacks were more visible in the second stage of involvement, competition, and confrontation. A brief history of grass-root neighborhood politics in Newark offers an explanation.

Since its inception, Newark has undergone several waves of immigrants and ethnic secessions in its politics. During the 1950s and 1960s Italian Americans dominated Newark politics. Gradually the Newark black population reached about 40%, and its black sub-community politics turned decidedly radical. Michael Parenti's work on the Newark Community Union Project (NCUP) illustrated this point. Over a three year period, black militants and their white allies (mainly Students for Democratic Society) mobilized the black community around building code enforcement and traffic lights. The group used all forms of protest ranging from rent strikes to sit-ins at a dangerous intersection needing a traffic light. All these efforts failed. Parenti suggested the powerlessness of the poor community make a mockery of pluralist theory which holds that any group can have their issues addressed if they organize themselves.[1] Newark city officials simply ignored the protest. This inaction further alienated the black population and may have contributed to the 1967 riot in Newark. A survey conducted by the Kerner Commission showed a low level of trust in local government among blacks, including those who did not participate in the riot.[2]

Meanwhile, Newark began losing population as the city's economic base shrank. An inevitable correlate of this decline was an eroding tax base and almost abandonment of the schools to the new minorities, blacks, and Puerto Ricans. By 1970, blacks were 54% of the city's population. Even after these dramatic population shifts, the legacy of de facto segregated schools remained.

Courts and De Facto Segregation

Newark schools were segregated because housing was separated by race and ethnicity. School authorities used the school attendance zones and transfer rules to prevent blacks from transferring to white schools. For example, in 1961 the board created a new school called Valisburg High School and promulgated a plan in which elementary students from the west side of 20th street were assigned to different schools than those on the east side. The east side black community believed that this plan was designed to prevent blacks from eventually transferring to Valisburg High. *Beale v. Board of Education of the City of Newark* (1961) was filed against the board of education. Judge Anthony Augelli asked the lawyers for both groups to try to make a settlement. The board agreed to use the optional pupil-transfer program that would allow black students to transfer to any school where there was space and also agreed to survey the system and to set up a citizen's advisory committee. The program began the next year and the parties agreed to drop the legal suit.

The so-called predominantly black schools were always thought to be inferior to those in other parts of the city. Prior to the lawsuit the Newark branch of the NAACP produced "A Report on Newark Public Schools" that documented the poor quality of education received by Newark black children. The report found that predominantly black elementary schools had a disproportional number of substitute teachers, no black supervisors, and an inadequate supply of textbooks. When the NAACP Education Committee approached the school board about remedies, they were rebuffed. The board claimed that "it does not initiate school activity or policy but merely acts on recommendations of the superintendent."[3] When the group approached the administrative staff, they got another negative response. "The staff stated that if there were problems in the schools, they would have corrected them. The NAACP Education Committee members were not 'professional educators,' and thus they are not qualified to judge the school system. The staff is gratified that the groups are interested in education in Newark, but the staff cannot and will be not stampeded into bowing to 'pressure groups'."[4] The type of treatment of outside groups was not limited to black groups. All types of groups took their grievances to the street.

Protesting Newark School Policy

There were several protests in the late 1960s. Phillip reported that between 1958 to 1972 there were 102 voluntary associations representing the black community before the board. By 1966 blacks and Puerto Ricans represented 74% of students in the schools.[5] The conflict over the racial integration and overcrowding of Newark schools divided the city. The involvement of the famous black nationalist playwright/community activist Amiri Baraka gave the school struggles high visibility in the metro-New York area. Anthony Imperiale, a city councilman, emerged as spokesperson for the working-class Italian Americans. At first glance it appeared to be a classic case of a black intellectual pitted against the forces of white conservatism. A closer look reveals a school cartel reacting swiftly to a threat to its powers.

In January of 1967, minorities were so underrepresented in school leadership positions that the Newark Civil Rights Commission demanded a black superintendent of schools and nondiscriminatory board hiring and promotion practices. Speakers at the January board meeting asserted that a black superintendent alone would understand the experience of black children and stop discrimination in school hiring revealed by the Commission's study.[6] Shortly thereafter, a heated controversy surrounded the replacement of Board Secretary Arnold Hess upon his announced resignation when Mayor Addonizio favored the apparently less-qualified Councilman James Callaghan (high school graduate) over black Budget Director Wilbur Parker, a CPA. One school activist stated "Some attribute the mayor's actions to racism. I say it was corruption. They wanted Callaghan because he would play ball. The Board Secretary handles all the hiring and purchasing. The Secretary determines who got the contracts. They didn't want Mr. Clean (Parker). This was my first realization of the school system as a boondoggle. Why the system was such a plum. The school system was a cash cow. They (city officials) were more interested in corruption as opposed to student learning."[7] This controversial statement was an eye-opener for the black community. The reaction to the Callaghan nomination was more than just a revolt against patronage, it also offended the sensibilities of the black middle class. Only Hess' decision to stay on could cool the controversy.

Blacks joined the legions of protesters over school policies. Among parent groups, the issues were overcrowded classrooms and integration. Among teachers, protest centered around safety issues. Newark schools reported two hundred and fifty assaults on teachers in a three-year span.[8] Only an agreement providing for police protection and a ban on outsiders entering school buildings averted an imminent teacher strike.

The infamous Vailsburg High School walkout occurred in May of 1968. Two hundred and fifty students combined a sit-down strike with a march outside of the school, demanding the reinstatement of five suspended white students and the exclusion of blacks who did not live in the predominately white Vailsburg area from the school.[9] The students had been suspended for a lunchroom fight with black students, which stemmed from an altercation the previous weekend over a white boy's dancing with a black girl. The conflict and the demonstration dramatized the racial tensions produced with the increased presence of black students. By 1968 busing and integration of northern public schools had become a national issue. The issue became so important that it emerged as a campaign issue in the 1968 presidential campaign.

A companion issue was decentralization of schools. The State Board of Education asked a committee, headed by Ruth Mancuso, to study redistricting of schools. Many Newark residents believed districting would eliminate racial boundaries that characterized all New Jersey schools. The Mancuso Report, released in June of 1968, was endorsed by then-State Education Commissioner Carl Marburger, who vowed to "lay my job on the line" to achieve complete racial integration of New Jersey public school children.[10] A proposal was made to convene a statewide urban education conference to discuss policy options. The Executive Director of Newark's Human Rights Commission, Harold Hodes, endorsed the idea, stating that the conference "should be prepared to reorganize and restructure the present system of education in the state."[11]

The Independent Board Members Association of New Jersey formed to combat the drive for racial parity. Newark board member John Cervase, repeatedly at odds with fellow board members, was elected as its first president. He called redistricting "a hoax to achieve forced racial integration through the back door."[12] The conference never took place despite the considerable support of Carole Graves of the Newark Teachers Union, Board President Harold Ashby, Newark teacher-activist Harry Wheeler, Sally Carroll of the Newark-Essex NAACP, and Newark teacher organizations.

State takeover of the Newark school district was proposed by Governor Richard Hughes's Select Commission on Civil Disorder, which was appointed following the summer of 1967 riots, during which 26 individuals were killed. The takeover plan was for five-year control, contingent upon acceptance by the Newark School Board. Anthony Imperiale of the North Ward Citizens Committee typified opposition sentiment, calling the plan a "governor's dictatorship"[13] While most participants opposed state takeovers of any aspect of school policy, the Organization of Negro Educators (ONE) opposed the takeover. They argued that blacks stood to inherit the nearly all-black schools in the near future.[14] Kenneth Gibson, a candidate in the 1966 mayoral election, voiced support of the temporary plan , as did the UAW.[15] The Commission also advocated decentralization of the Newark school authority. Meanwhile white flight continued, and more minorities moved into previous all-white neighborhoods.

Black and Brown Schools

Although black children became the dominant ethnic group in the schools in the late 1960s, whites still governed the schools as they always had. The city still has strong Italian neighborhoods on the north side, Forest Hills, and a Portuguese population in the eastern Ironbound section. Although the Puerto Rican population was also increasing, its leaders were not well known. The 1970 census documented the shift of the population within the city and into the surrounding area. Whites were resettling in the outer suburbs, the New Jersey shores and Sussex County. Blacks were moving outside the central ward of Newark into other neighborhoods. Some residents moved to Essex County, Hillside, and Irvingon.

Between 1965-76, the Board of Education steered a course through troubled waters, guided by no master plan. Analysis of board minutes discloses that five strategies were utilized: 1) granting some requests that were peripheral to education but were used to satisfy the political needs of the Board of Education, such as changing the names of schools to conform with neighborhood ethnicity; 2) ignoring demands whenever possible, even though this could mean chaos and violence at public meetings; 3) impaneling a commission or citizens' advisory group to recommend changes in management or administration, sex education, curriculum, student rights, or healing divisions after a strike; 4) pleading that no funds are available for new programs; and, 5) if necessary, funding new programs with federal money. There was no marked difference between the responses of the black- and white-dominated Boards of Education. Meanwhile the politics of the city were changing. The grass-roots black nationalist movement had mobilized Newark residents into a viable political force. Blacks were now ready to assume to take political control from the Italian Americans. In 1966 Gerald Pomper, a voting behavior expert, found that in non-partisan elections ethnic voters voted for candidates from their own ethnic group.[16] Ethnic identification didn't elect Gibson in the 1966 election, but after the 1967 riots, racial solidarity among Newark black voters became a mobilizing force.

The Election of Kenneth Gibson

The 1970 election of Kenneth A. Gibson to the mayoralty in Newark was a major step in the development of black politics in the northeastern city. Having been nominated by the Black and Puerto Rican Convention founded by black nationalist Amiri Imamu Baraka (the former LeRoi Jones) and Robert Curvin (then of CORE), Gibson's background as a civil engineer and his reputation as a moderate reformer facilitated the cooperation among the various political factions in black factions in Newark. Gibson's opponent, Hugh Addonizio, who had a reputation for corruption and was the subject of a criminal investigation at that time, was an easy target for his campaign.

Despite the efforts of a well-oiled political machine, Gibson, who had run unsuccessfully in 1966, led a field of seven in the primary with 40% of the vote, outdistancing the sitting mayor Addonizio and conservative Anthony Imperiale. The runoff between Gibson and Addonizio witnessed a rather open appeal to racial fears. Addonizio attempted to link Gibson to Baraka's brand of black nationalism. Gibson repeatedly indicated that he would not appoint Baraka to any position within his administration. Fortunately for Gibson, the federal district attorney's case against Addonizio generated incessant negative publicity, and the mayor was eventually sent to jail.

In the 1970 campaign Gibson used education issues to highlight his progressive posture. He pledged to campaign on a platform that included community control of schools. Accordingly, he promised to consult with teachers before making appointments to the board and to meet with NTU leaders and other city unions once a month to discuss any issues that might come up.[17] He asserted about the board: "My revising of the Board of Education will encompass selecting qualified people, both black and white, who can relate to the needs of the people—especially to the needs of our children. . . . That is one of the main problems we have today—the needs of our children are ignored, with many members of the Board of Education being unable to relate to them."[18] Accordingly, he asserted that Newark teachers weren't properly trained to cope with the problems they had to confront in the city's schools. Gibson also expressed his opposition to busing because it wasn't cost effective given the majority-black enrollment in the schools.

At the time of his election, the city had a 54 % black population. Gibson won by 12,000 votes. Election results showed Gibson unexpectedly receiving white votes in the Italian American North Ward. Robert Curvin observed,

> The election of Kenneth A. Gibson as mayor of Newark represented a profound change in the political leadership of that city. It was not only a shift from white power to Black power, although, on the surface, this was perhaps the most significant aspect of his victory.

It was much deeper than that. Gibson rode to victory in front of a mass movement of Blacks, aided by an interracial force of reformers. Civil rights activists, young and old idealists and the fiery Black nationalist, Imamu Baraka, and his followers, were all united in forging Gibson's victory. Gibson entered office with a broad base of public support. He pledged to correct long standing social wrongs, to improve services, end corruption, and achieve new effectiveness in government.[19]

In his first State of the City address, the mayor asserted, "Education is the first priority of this Administration, and yet education is the one single area where we have been least able to accomplish our objectives." Gibson then articulated three of what he described as "obtainable objectives." He designated the next school year as "Right to Read Year."[20]

The mayor was a product of the Newark school system. Arriving in Newark in 1940 from Enterprise, Alabama, he found himself ahead of his fellow students at a time when Newark schools were considered among the best in the nation. "I was at least one year ahead of all other students. I came out of a little pot belly school in Enterprise, Alabama. I taught half of my class. I was barred from participation in spelling matches because it was unfair to the other kids."[21] Gibson graduated from Cleveland Junior High in 1947 and Central High School in 1950. He also attended the Newark College of Engineering (now called New Jersey Institute of Technology). The future mayor became a structural engineer for the city. As a parent, Gibson never attended the PTA meetings, but as a politician he wanted to "do something about the schools."[22]

The new mayor appointed an Education Task Force, with a full-time professional staff, to review board procedures. Gibson also pleaded to support the state's Chancellor Plan to create a graduate center in Newark. He began to appoint more black members to the board, consistent with the racial composition of the schools. The first ideological crisis of the Gibson Administration came after the board decided to allow schools with black majorities to display the Black Liberation flag. This issue divided the black community and pitted the black nationalists against the old leadership of the Urban League. The mayor did not let himself get caught up in this controversial issue and eventually the issue died.

The Great School Strike

The ascendancy of Gibson came at a time when there was turmoil between the teacher unions and the board. The Newark Teachers Union replaced the Newark Teacher Association as the sole bargaining unit for teachers in 1969. Carole Graves, a black special education teacher, was elected president in 1969, quickly becoming a major force in the hostile school politics arena. The combination of a dismantled Addonizio machine and Gibson's reform claims created a window of opportunity for the increasingly militant teachers' union.

Graves led a three week successful strike against the schools in February of 1970. The board agreed to a contract that gave the union some veto power over school policy. After the board attempted to renege on some of the language later in that year, Ms. Graves took her people to the street again. This time, the whole affair resulted in a media blitz lasting from February to April of 1971. The strike centered around board opposition to binding arbitration and the implementation of contract provisions freeing teachers from non-professional chores and promising a welfare fund of $400 per teacher. In total, 55 days of school were lost. Catch-up efforts were attempted, such as the Victoria Plan at the Cleveland School, which provided one million dollars, but results were mixed.[23]

The entire community was angry over the handling of the strike. Cervase publicly claimed that "outside forces" were influencing the board's handling of the strike and was branded a "liar" by then-president Jesse Jacob, who said Cervase should "not in any way speak for this board, now or ever."[24] Reverend Henry Cade, chairman of the Newark Community Coalition, called an attempt at voluntary school sessions at the end of March a "sham or game" designed by the board and the NTU for compensating striking teachers. After the strike, parents kept 80 to 100 returning teachers from their classrooms on Maple Avenue and South Eighth Street schools. Then, the five-person Board of School Estimates rejected the board's emergency request for $2.1 million because board secretary Hess had inadequately documented the need for it, according to Gibson and Councilman Sharpe James. School officials welcomed immediate outside assistance. That fall, Gibson announced his desire for a probe of school board funds, even if it resulted in legislation calling for a restructuring of the system.

During the strike Gibson met a seventeen-year-old black high school student and track star named Larry Hamm. Hamm had led a demonstration to reopen the schools. He was not taking sides in the crisis. He struck Gibson as a very bright young man with strong opinions. Gibson decided to appoint Hamm to the Board of Education. "We looked up the law and there is no prohibition on age. I called him in and told him that I wanted to appoint him. I told him he would go from obscurity to national prominence. Don't let it go to your head. Whatever you do don't quit school."[25] The novel idea of appointing a young person with recent knowledge of school life to the school board backfired against the new mayor. The mayor never appointed another young person to the board after Hamm. Meanwhile, the Mayor's problems were just beginning.

Hamm received a scholarship from Princeton, but within three months he quit college. According to former mayor Gibson, Leroi Jones captured him.

> He changed his name to Adhimu Chunga and demanded that the names of the schools be changed to reflect black heroes. Why change names? Why change Robert Treat, the founder of Newark? You can't change history by changing names. He also wanted the Black Liberation Flag outside every school. I opposed him.[26]

This era in Newark history may have been the peak of LeRoi Jones' influence in school policy or for that matter in Newark politics. The public school establishment would wait him out rather than try to confront him directly.

Another Crisis

The resolution of the Great Strike brought about only temporary relief to the school crisis in Newark. The push for decentralization became stronger during the 1970 and 1971 strike negotiations. Council President Louis Turco and board member Dr. Michael Petti urged during the 1971 strike that local boards be created representing each of the five wards to change the current configuration into an advisory central board. Charles Bell, a former union organizer who became school board president in 1970, championed moderate "community committees" to prevent the undue influence of small organized groups on board decisions.[27] Gibson continued his opposition to any such transfer of authority. He stated in one television appearance,

> So what actually do we mean by community participation? Who selects the community participants? You really can't expect a housewife to determine what's going to happen in a mathematics curriculum situation. . . . I'm opposed to assuming that because you have a child in school then you can determine what's going to happen in the school system[28]

The state Superior Court voided the five three-year-old associate superintendent positions on December 17 after the board could not meet the requirements of a show-cause order obtained by the mayor the prior week. Gibson criticized the spending, claiming that the board must "have a more effective system of control on spending decisions." Cervase added that "they are a luxury we cannot afford considering the fiscal crisis" of the time.[29]

Despite the mayor's and board's resistance, parental agitation for acknowledgment by school officials continued. Parents forced teacher transfers at (the former Southside High) Malcolm X. Shabazz High School. This was the location of the city's lone "School Within a School" (SWAS) program for the gifted (hailed as a "success"), when board leaders urged "voluntary" transfers to avoid possible violence by PTSA members.[30] Vailsburg was again boycotted, in one of the most notorious incidents of the system's history, when white students protested the reassignment of a teacher alleged to be harsher on black students than whites. The Concerned Vailsburg Community Committee, chaired by former mayoral candidate Anthony Imperiale, achieved a formalized role for the community in the school's staff reassignment decisions. This occurred much to the chagrin of board member Adhimu Chunga, the 19-year-old Black Nationalist Lawrence Hamm.[31] The agreement meant reinstatement of the teacher, a black man.

The mayor's 27-member Task Force emerged as "one of the most important influences" in school policy after the strike.[32] The executive system was revamped to enlarge the power of the superintendent as a result of the panel's analysis of school authority. Because the business manager, the board secretary, and the school superintendent had direct lines to the board, authority was unclear and administration was inefficient. The school's cartel response to this indictment was to acquiesce to the appointment of a black superintendent.

A Black Superintendent

In July of 1973 Stanley Taylor was appointed the district's first black superintendent. Chosen out of 31 candidates, Taylor was an experienced district superintendent of Community Board #13 in Brooklyn. He succeeded Dr. Edward I. Pfeffer who had been acting superintendent for a year. Hugh Scott described the situation that Taylor faced.

> For many years, the role of superintendent in Newark was diluted by the direct activities of members of the board and by the involvement of city hall in the administration of public education. Also, the structural, organizational relationship of certain key school officials called for their reporting, not to the superintendent, but to the board. Politics and education in Newark had been intimately commingled prior to the arrival of Mayor Kenneth Gibson. Taylor moved in a very disciplined manner to effect the organizational changes needed to establish the appropriate administrative coverage for the office of the superintendent.[33]

Describing Taylor as "patiently aggressive" with staff and diplomatic with his board, Scott found him upbeat after being on the job for six months. However, he constantly defended himself against the local so-called militants. Militants would turn out to be a small problem for Taylor.

The first major fiscal crisis for the new superintendent and the new mayor came at the end of the 1974-75 school year. There was a $35 million system deficit. Gibson proposed a $17 million cut in school spending to reduce the deficit. The mayor believed that a redistribution of the state education fund, advocated by Governor Brendan Bryne, would have wiped out the city budget. Taylor proposed layoffs of 1600 teachers and other board employees—those not involved in central office administration. The Newark Board eventually approved a $129 million budget for the 1975-76 school year, calling for the termination of 1,116 jobs. The number of teachers would be reduced by 12%. Carole Graves, still president of the teacher's union, attacked the board's action. She called the whole affair an attempt to put pressure on the state legislature to pass an income tax increase.

Several hundred high school students demonstrated at Newark City Hall and at the board office to protest the cuts. A five-day boycott by students occurred in the schools of the traditional, union-supportive Ironbound section. This area was home to the Independence High successful program for delinquents and created another political crisis. To add to this, 250 parents and students led by Imamu Amiri Baraka rallied at City Hall on May 14, 1975.

School board President Charles Bell attacked the superintendent's management of the situation. Taylor, who had placed a $15,000 order for office furniture the previous fall (from which he cut $1,183 when the news generated extremely negative publicity), met with Baraka. Baraka also met with Walter Wechsler. Wechsler was appointed by the state Department of Education in February of 1975 to head a task force reviewing school fiscal affairs. Charles Bell acted to defuse the issue, getting the board members to rescind the layoff notices despite the deficit. The students returned to class.

Bell openly feuded with Taylor in the fall, after Taylor announced that he had reorganized top administrative staff. The plan—unilaterally implemented—split the board along certain ideological lines. Bell became angry and questioned the legality of taking such steps without consulting the board. Board members Branch, Fullilove, Means, and Donaldson claimed that the move was discussed with them after a walkout of other members from a board meeting. Like Bell, Carol Graves was angered and sent a letter to him asking for charges to be filed against Taylor. This public bickering eroded the public image of all the people involved.

A Threatened State Takeover

The fiscal crisis resurrected the issue of state intervention into the Newark district, setting forces in motion for outside involvement. Gibson continued to support the State Board of Education's efforts. He supported a state Senate-passed measure for restructured school financing in the face of strong opposition led by the Greater Newark Urban Coalition. At the same time, the reorganizing legislation called for the assignment of a state-appointed overseer, an "auditor general," an action credited in large part to his leadership.[34] This major reform effort, which was largely a product of Wechsler's six-month review, created the executive superintendent post along with that of the auditor general.

The thirty-one-year old Thomas Marshello entered Newark politics stressing that he was not part of a state takeover. He described his auditor general position as an "objective appraiser of the quality of board business operations" and indicated that the board "still maintains its integrity as a semi-autonomous body."[35] At the end of 1976, State Education Commissioner Fred Burke was claiming success for the arrangement in "resolving bonding problems, speeding up audit reporting, placing 'strict controls' on payroll and creating a 'professional' personnel department." Board resentment continued, with Helen Fullilove calling the auditor general "a white overseer," and President Carl Dawson, a Gibson aide, calling Burke's claim "misleading."[36]

The release of the Caputo Report in February of 1977 further elaborated state concerns about Newark schools. Authored by former Essex County Schools Superintendent Ralph Caputo, the special report on the condition of Newark schools documented unsafe and unsanitary conditions in numerous city schools. A special Urban Education Team was designated to explore the problem, and a remedial plan was implemented by the district for its correction. This plan contained 101 objectives for the remediation of deficiencies in educational and supportive services. School officials were given one year to improve. In addition, NTU officials charged in May that the board had misused funds taken under the State Compensatory Education program. A letter to the State Education Department contended that there was no evidence of student enrollment in such a program or compensation to teachers, because the funds supplemented general board operations rather than existing educational programming.[37]

Reviews of Stanley Taylor's administration were mixed. In the beginning of March, eight members of the council cast a vote of "no confidence" against the Executive Superintendent. Parents had positive feelings about his administration, decrying the council move in a meeting with Board President Sharif and Council President Earl Harris in the mayor's office. PTA members were positive that individual accountability had increased under the administration at that time. Board president Carl Sharif (formerly Carl Dawson) followed up on the meeting with a proposal for mandatory parent orientation programs in April.

Any optimism about the schools dissipated as tension and controversy were renewed in 1978. Gibson suggested at public hearings that teachers needed to be monitored, advocating evaluations of teacher performance and better attendance for teachers as well as students.[38] The Essex County Prosecutor launched two grand jury investigations in August, inquiring into ballooning construction costs for East Side High School additions and the spending practices of officials of the federally-funded Title I program. Continuing fiscal problems reached a head with drastic teacher layoffs at the end of the year.

In January of 1979 3,500 teachers boycotted schools along with non-instructional staff after the last 277 of these layoffs took effect. Remaining teachers were expected to do jobs once performed by dismissed non-instructional workers, and slight modifications in educational programs altered normal work responsibilities. NTU leadership supported state help for the district, saying that something was wrong and "we will not work under those conditions."[39] The crisis appeared to be as intense as any known by Newark, as Carol Graves broke down in tears at a crowded public meeting with a state Board of Education. She demanded the suspension of the board, recision of the layoff order, and an investigation. A strike was averted, but educational disruption was not over as schools closed during the negotiations in March.

> Teacher contentions that the situation was unworkable were bolstered by the White-Burcat report, which soberly identified seventy areas of deficiency in the Newark school system. The "finding letter," written by the Essex County Superintendent and appointed monitor, warned that progress in meeting objectives designated in the remedial plan was inadequate in rate and content. This threatened Newark district compliance with state criteria for "approved" district status per the 1975 reform legislation.[40]

Realignment of Mayoral Powers in the Schools

In 1971 Gibson opposed a plan to decentralize the school board and the idea of an elected board. In 1973 the mayor criticized a black board member for inciting blacks in the Vailsburg incident. The mayor's solution to the problem was to appoint new members to the Board of Education. Mayor Gibson appointed an ethnic mix on the Board of Education: a black majority, a single Puerto Rican, and four whites.

Gibson's first Board of Education was described by *The New York Times* as "middle class." Gibson's board now included blacks of many different social classes. He had been careful to reappoint white representatives and represent white districts. Gibson had, since 1973, been less prone to shift white Board of Education members than blacks after their first three-year term. By 1976

Gibson's appointments reflected a new pattern: both black and white appointees to the Board of Education tended to be connected to city agencies. In 1977 it became clear these appointments provided the mayor with more leverage for political control.[41] In the same year the system's first black superintendent Stanley Taylor was dismissed. In 1978 Alonzo Kittrels was officially appointed the new school executive superintendent.

The rift between the mayor and union leaders had reached its pinnacle when Graves threatened a mass mailing to recall Gibson. Gibson had begun his third mayoral term in 1978 with strong concern for education, voicing the opinion that racial tension had subsided and various groups were working together. In the early 1980s, however, he was not optimistic in assessing his ability to solve the difficult problems challenging schools: "We are only given certain powers. Very limited power in dealing with education to avoid the whole question of patronage and the politicians controlling curriculum and that kind of thing."[42] He was described in another television interview as "sober" in his assessment of his powers with the school board.

> I appoint the members of the Board for three year staggered terms. . . . Appoint three each year. Once you appoint them, they are there for three years. I can't remove them. Many people that I have appointed—I shouldn't say many—some of the people that I have appointed changed their policies after being appointed. I can't remove them. It's an autonomous board. I do not sign the contract with the Newark Teachers' Union. The Board of Education does that. They negotiate those contracts. We try to influence them. Sometimes they listen to us. Sometimes they don't.[43]

In actuality, the mayor was probably at the zenith of his power in education policy during this period. His rift with the teacher's union continued to grow. In February of 1979 Gibson was scheduled to teach a course in urban problems at the New School in New York and 75 protesters showed up to greet him.

Union influence in city politics continued to grow in absence of a strong local political party. Yet Gibson, because of his popularity, was able to keep the union at bay. However, the replacement of Superintendent Alonzo Kittrels in 1981 led to a showdown over a wayward board appointment that exposed the power wielded by the mayor. The attempt to enter the third stage of black involvement in school politics, consolidation and routinization, had failed, and a realignment of power eventuated.

Upon taking office, Mayor Gibson adopted a practice that required each of his appointees to the board to sign a resignation letter at the beginning of their three-year term. Brenda Grier had her resignation announced for her at a September board meeting, after she opposed the mayor's hand-picked candidate and asked board attorneys to review procedures used in the vote approving him. She challenged the action.

Grier cited the appointment of Columbus Salley to the superintendency, the fifth- or sixth-ranked of ten finalists, in her appeal to the State commissioner of education for redress. She said she and other board members were instructed to vote for Salley hours before he was named, with Gibson claiming "the board is made up of nine members and I'm the tenth."[44] Her petition also asserted that Sharif's membership on the school board represented a conflict because of his employment as a mayoral aide. Ms. Grier was reinstated to her seat seven months later. The judge cited legislative intent (i.e., separation of mayoral and board powers) as the reason for not granting the mayor his claims for a pre-resignation letter. To allow this kind of practice would increase the mayor's power over the Board.

The controversy dogged Salley as he took office. West Ward Councilman Michael Bottone sponsored a resolution deploring the circumstances of the superintendent's selection as an embarrassment subjecting the city to "ridicule and question across this nation." Salley declared "I'm not a politician. I'm an educator" and "I won't let anyone shackle our schools with failure and mediocrity."[45] His tenure was marked by the shadow of excessive mayoral power. Salley later characterized Kenneth Gibson as "second to none in educational enlightenment."[46]

Newark voters adopted a referendum to elect school board members, engineered by a strongly union-backed group of citizens on May 11, 1982. A *Star-Ledger* special edition attributed the final push for an elected board to the Grier ouster.[47] In August 1971, Council President Louis Turco had sponsored a resolution calling for an elected board. Councilman Sharpe James and Mayor Kenneth Gibson were the most vocal opponents, claiming that the move was racial given Newark's history of minority under-representation in government positions, especially elected offices. The full council tabled the resolution after Gibson sent it a letter appealing to fears of racial polarization. Anger about the 1981 power struggle led to renewal of the elected school board drive, with the perception of administrative chaos and evidence that educational quality was poor and pointed to political abuse.

East Ward Councilman Henry Martinez assembled a special council committee at this time to investigate the entire board's operation. A week before it formally convened, Salley called a press conference to tout the "ecology of excellence" prevailing under his administration. He identified several successful programs: a truancy task force credited by school and police officials for a 10% increase in attendance and a 30% decrease in street crime; homework assistance centers; and a "Newark students will succeed" campaign.[48] Daniel Gibson, a mayor appointee and no relation to the mayor, cites the period between 1981-1984 as the "most productive period" in Newark school history. He attributes this to the joint efforts of the board members and Superintendent Salley. Board member Gibson asserted

> During this period there was a quantum leap in district wide test math and reading scores for children. There was 17% increase in reading scores and a 20% increase in math scores. The results were staggering. The state board of education delayed certifying the numbers pending an investigation. They want to know if the district cheated.[49]

The scores were valid but that did not stop the criticism of the board or the superintendent. Carol Graves assailed Salley for his exclusion of union officials from matters affecting teachers such as textbooks selection. She claimed that her membership was "unhappy" with board affairs, including its failure to constructively negotiate a new contract.

The entire school cartel was apprehensive about the city council's investigation of the school management. Salley was especially defensive, publicly lambasting the City Council committee as "more political than fact-finding" and "deliberately misleading" in charges of mismanagement.[50] He asserted that his administration had restored fiscal integrity to budget-making, which was beset with deficits under Kittrel's leadership.

Salley also encountered problems with the union when the board imposed the Attendance Improvement Plan (AIP). This program was intended to improve the class attendance of Newark teachers. Salley announced the program's success after attendance increased 23.3% over the previous year (1982). Salley concluded, "Not only does this reverse a 10-year trend in teacher attendance, it also represents a financial saving of almost a half a million dollars in substitute cost and the addition of 60,000 hours or almost 11,000 days when students and teachers are productively interacting." Graves disagreed, stating "I can say in general the AIP has not been a success. It has created more problems than it has resolved."[51] In January 1983 the NTU filed an unfair labor practice suit against the board over AIP.

In the early 1980s Gibson's influence over board affairs greatly diminished. In March of 1982 he was touched by scandal when he was named in an indictment charging that he gave former Councilman Michael Bontempo a "no-show" job. The trial ended in a hung jury and a mistrial was declared. Although the indictment was thrown out, the mayor's reputation had clearly taken some heavy blows. In May, he was forced to relinquish his power of appointment with a referendum on board elections. In June, he barely achieved a fourth mayoral term in a close election against Earl Harris (52% to 48%). For a man who had finished third in a field of 13 candidates for Governor just a year earlier, the close race meant he was losing his grip on his constituency.

Elected Board and Union Power

The 1982 election which changed the board from an appointed to an elected one was a major change in Newark school politics. Councilman Donald Tucker thought that the switch to the elected board represented a "downhill spiral" in Newark school politics. "When the board was appointed by the mayor, the people knew who to hold accountable. Who do you hold accountable with an elected board?" He continued,

> Instead of looking at the funding mechanism and teacher accountability, the board started to deal with governance. The question became who is in charge. Governance began to overshadow other issues. The community activists controlled who gets on the board. This had nothing to do with the parents. We have 300,000 people in Newark and only 7,000 people vote in [school] elections. That is less than 5% of the registered voters.[52]

In this case, low turnout could be viewed as a deliberate election tactic by the Newark school cartel. The fewer the number of voters, the less costly are campaigns. Over time, this small voting population could be identified and targeted. After the first election, the task for the cartel was how to manage the transition. Since members serve staggered terms, the real political changes could not take effect until all board members were elected.

One of the most controversial issues to come before the mixed board of appointed and elected members was the tenure of Carl Sharif, the president. Some community activists supported the reelection of Sharif, who had to be reaffirmed as president within thirty days of his "holdover" appointment to the board. Baraka, who chaired an impromptu meeting when the board left for a three-hour private session, was preoccupied with mayoral influence in the system. A rift had reportedly developed between the mayor and Sharif, his aide, just as it had years earlier between the mayor and Baraka. Speakers supported the board's reelection of Sharif, who was beset with his own troubles, including an attempted murder charge for which he was acquitted. The process of voting caused an uproar and security guards had to stand in front of the members as they voted. The board voted (6-2) to oust Carl Sharif from the presidency. Delores McNeil was elected president.

At the same meeting Superintendent Salley's contract was extended. Carole Graves exploded at the news of the extension of Salley's contract. "This is a violation of the spirit and intent of the Sunshine law. You ought to be ashamed of yourself. How dare you? Are you crazy? This is undemocratic. This action is a scourge upon the city."[53]

Graves castigated outsiders such as Essex County Superintendent Elena Scambio, a former board member in Newark and a Gibson appointee, and State Education Commissioner Saul Cooperman. She called for the termination of Board Counsel Rosen for his failure to inform board members of the need to vote promptly on the presidency question: "Whether we were against each other in the past, and whether we may be against each other in the future, no one should come in and call the shots in the Newark school system."[54]

Despite the fact the union dominated the discourse on schools, there was real discontent which could have led to a new surge of school protest in the community. To obviate this possibility the teachers union sponsored a group of candidates running under the banner of "People United for Better Schools" (PUBS). PUBS was formed in 1983 by those who had mobilized for the elected board referendum, with the slogan "quality education through community involvement." Its platform supported an "independent board that has authority to determine its own agenda and hire its (own) staff to carry out responsibilities."[55] Charles Bell, with Sharif and Kittrels, managed the campaign of its three candidates, who were the top three finishers in an election in which fewer than 9,000 votes were cast.

PUBS filed a complaint with the State Education Department after the board would not certify its winning candidates in favor of the fourth and fifth Gibson-endorsed finishers. The board argued that Reverend Oliver Brown and Edgar Brown, Jr., were disqualified from holding board positions by a lawsuit they filed against the board fighting a Salley contract extension. Gibson was implicated in the dispute, despite his protests that "I have no legal authority over the board. Frankly, I am not sure if I told any board members anything that they would do what I told them, anyway."[56] An administrative law judge ruled on April 25 that the board had acted improperly and that the top vote-getting candidates should be seated.

Gibson faulted the election process because of the low voters turnout, denying that his candidates' losses signified political problems for him. He added that voter rejection of the budget meant that the budget question still had not been determined by direct vote. At the same time, City Council President Ralph Grant enthusiastically commented, "I have great confidence that the three new members . . . can work together . . . so that some of the constant confrontation on the board of education can be put behind us."[57]

The first item on the new members' agenda was the removal of Columbus Salley from administrative office. The new majority voted in June to suspend him with pay for incompetence, after which Salley acquired a restraining order preventing them from taking actions directed at his firing before a hearing scheduled for January 1985. Eugene Campbell, Kittrels' deputy, was named acting superintendent. The board did not settle the issue until November 1985, when it agreed to pay Salley $660,000 to buy out his contract. However, the settlement marked the end of the third stage of black involvement, the consolidation and routinization of political power.

That August the school board shocked officials with a precedent-setting three-year contract agreement with the NTU. The pact granted salary increases totaling 23% over the three years, promising pay increases to individuals taking equivalency courses to be run by the union. It also included a provision allowing union officials to exclude school administrators from classrooms while they conducted "observations" of teachers. Gibson reacted strongly. He accused the board of "surrendering its management prerogatives," and denounced PUBS members' role in the contract as a "blatant" attempt to repay the union for its support in their election. Graves, whose organization had helped in PUBS campaigns, referred to them as "our candidates."[58]

The mayor pointed out the limits of his power with respect to board decisions: "All I can do is raise hell. If they are going to turn over the shop, then let them say that they are going to turn over the shop."[59] Sharpe James, member of the City Council, called for an emergency meeting to discuss the implications of the agreement. The reality was that the union had won and any criticism was considered an attack on the school system. Gibson was attacked in a black weekly. "The political hoopla is not concerned with education. Historically Mayor Gibson has maintained a posture against raises for educators. He expresses concern for education but it has never been a number one priority."[60]

Gibson asked state officials for assistance in changing the agreement. Gibson's request for state assistance amounted to an admission that he had less influence over the board. The local newspaper pointed out the irony of the situation. When Gibson controlled the board, he did not want any outside interference. Now that the union controlled the board, he was seeking outside help. State officials, who were cautious in their immediate responses to the agreement, pressured the parties into dropping the provision for union-exclusive "observation" and modifying the provision for union-run credited courses to grant full authority over their administration to the board. Saul Cooperman made an announcement concerning the unprecedented state involvement, that "school districts should know I will be willing to act if I believe contract provisions violate educational law."[61]

At this time, the state was involved in Newark affairs in the monitoring process as well. At a board meeting spurred by the state's June proposal to intervene in school districts that were deficient, Campbell (named Executive Superintendent in December 1985) announced that the district still fell short of state requirements at the end of the 1985-86 school year. New Jersey Education officials evaluated districts in eleven areas, and at three levels of monitoring, before state takeovers of local operations could be proposed. Newark fell short of the requirements under

Level 2 monitoring in three of these areas: student attendance, professional staffing, and high school proficiency test scores. Citizen reaction to the possibility of state takeover was not all negative. The decline of Gibson's influence in school politics was matched by the perception that he had been in power too long. After an unsuccessful gubernatorial candidacy, Gibson was now open to a serious challenge. It came from his ally in the city council, Sharpe James.

The Election of Sharpe James

The overwhelming perception of trouble in Newark school leadership was part of Sharpe James' successful campaign to unseat Gibson. While James disputed Gibson's contention that "education is the key concern," he did not fail to point out that

> The city's schools, over which the mayor had direct control under two years ago, are a disaster . . . the current administration has exercised a policy of confrontation as opposed to education. For 12 years Mayor Gibson appointed every board of education member and then had them sign undated letters of resignation so that he could "retire" them when they sought to exercise their own personal judgment. . . . No mayor can order the board of education to name his choice for superintendent of schools without accepting the charge of political interference in the educational process.[62]

James at this time voiced his support of the election of school board members. He pushed citizen responsibility in school governance. James also attacked the fiscal management of schools. "You learn of the budget and then learn students are without supplies. I don't think we're getting our dollar's worth as far as the quality of curriculum."[63] Reverend Oliver Brown, also a candidate, defended the proposed budget on the basis of the district's size and relatively low per-student expenditure, which he contended was $2,000 vs. upwards of $6,000 in the suburbs. Board member Reverend Oliver Brown was the eventual third-place candidate. Sharpe James easily defeated Gibson on May 13,

1986. James' election could have come at an inauspicious time for Newark and the nation. The country had seen six years of Reagan conservatism and some liked his tilt away from the problems of the inner city. James faced even more of a challenge than when Gibson assumed the mayoralty.

The conflictual board politics continued under the James Administration. A schism developed in the board, as all nine members were PUBS-backed since the April election. Four members led by Reverend Oliver Brown declared their intention to refuse to vote on non-emergency matters because of the old problem of timely and complete information. The protest bloc prepared a statement calling for receipt of contracts and resolutions one month in advance—a performance analysis of all consultants, vendors, and contractors; a cost analysis showing their respective economic impacts; information from the legal department 45 days in advance of deadlines; and action on administrative appointments within one month of their announcement. They thwarted action on the July and August agendas.

Charles Bell, again board president, warned that the members' "showboating" was playing into the hands of proponents of a state takeover. The board was instructed in a letter from Essex County Superintendent Scambio to take action on various lagging administrative items at the September meeting. They did so in a two-hour executive session on September 23.

The board finally prepared a contract offer for Executive Superintendent Campbell, who had been without a contract since the previous winter. Scambio warned that the offer in the face of an unfavorable evaluation of his performance was a "state concern" because the "district is not certified and we have a responsibility for assuring those actions are taken that would lead to it."[64] The offer of a two-year contract, retroactive, was approved anyway. The specter of state supervision hovered over the system's ongoing education problems, prompting Mayor James to decry the "deteriorated" system in his first State of the City message to the Greater Newark Chamber of Commerce.

The mayor used the opportunity to request a return to the appointed board form, stating that he would meet with city council members to work out a method by which appointment powers could be shared. He now advocated placing "education as the top priority" for the city, with the entire community "working in partnership."[65] Bell agreed on the priority of educational problems and maximal community involvement in their solution but disputed the deterioration of the system, pointing to significant improvements in reading and math scores in the just-completed school year. Bell also asserted, "The electoral process maximizes the possible participation of all who want to vote. And you need maximum participation to have a good school system."[66]

Graves of the NTU allowed, "and as for the people who criticize the low voter turnouts, I would ask them what they did to motivate more people to come out and vote." She predicted "it will be very hard to change something that diminished the rights of people to vote."[67] In July, the board was bombarded with representatives of community organizations pleading for improvement in state-monitored areas. The Newark Panel for Educational Priorities (NPEP), a coalition including the Newark branch of the NAACP and the Essex County Urban League, specifically criticized the lack of consistency with maintaining principals, a "fat" senior administrative staff that was not evaluated on a consistent basis, and the lack of results delivered by leaders. The head of the Newark Coalition for Neighborhoods (NCN) reiterated the theme of failed leadership, adding that "a clear philosophy of education and purpose is critical."[68] A spokesman for the Greater Newark Renaissance Group called for a rationale for central office job functions, school personnel evaluations, and annual community reports with fiscal, administrative, and educational data. Speakers demanded that they be included in major policy decisions, accusing the board of frustrating their attempts at staying informed and forming a voice.

A special board meeting was held on August 12, 1987 to respond to these demands. The board agreed to a review of the system's management operations, of which the NPEP and other groups wanted to be a working part. The board pointed to its involvement in a three-year program of educational improvement at that time, the duration of which the NPEP termed "kind of ludicrous" for a multi-million dollar system. The president of the Vailsburg High PTA said that attending meetings with school officials was "depressing" because of the lack of results. Former Board President Carl Sharif, affiliated with the Greater Newark Renaissance Group, concurred that he was concerned "about whether or not they'll follow through and take any of this stuff seriously." Campbell promised the groups that he would issue an edict to school principals ordering them to "maximize their meetings with the community and parents."[69] The board scheduled another meeting for the following week.

The community's mood of pessimism at this time was validated by the county superintendent's report on the status of the district. However, the mobilization of the community was rewarded to some degree as well. Scambio asserted that student and staff attendance rates and student test scores were not high enough to warrant leniency from the state. But she stated that it was "premature to talk about state intervention in Newark," asserting that "the district should get special consideration."[70] State Commissioner Saul Cooperman expressed optimism that there was a "strong image of success in urban education" after his tour of the schools in December.[71] There were some grounds for optimism in the area of school-community collaboration.

In May 1987 Superintendent Campbell announced the School and Business Partnership Program that would establish a cooperative relationship for each of the city's public schools. He stated that "twenty to thirty percent of our schools are now involved in some type of partnership; our goal is to make that 100 percent."[72] A panel created in October of 1987 to facilitate discussion of educational issues and implement plans announced an initiative expanding the school-business partnership plan. Under this plan a corporation would "adopt" a school in a target neighborhood to address its specific needs. This was the Newark Education Council, designed to expand on collaborative efforts among parents, school leaders, the private sector, and the state.[73]

However, the state takeover threat was ever present. Deficiencies uncovered in the third year of state monitoring were discussed at a public forum in May of 1988. County Superintendent

Scambio recommended that the Newark district not be accredited on the basis of its deficiencies in 17 of 54 areas evaluated. Problems included failure to meet minimum standards for teacher and student attendance, failure to provide an updated curriculum, and failure to make necessary structural repairs to facilities, the cost of which Charles Bell estimated at $180 million.[74]

Mayor James' second State of the City address was downbeat about the schools. "The quality of education in the Newark school system has not kept pace with rising administrative costs, especially the layers and layers of administrative personnel and non-instructional costs." He emphasized again that he attributed the downward spiral to the election of board members, calling for a return to mayoral appointment. He pointed out that "less than 9 percent of Newark's population participates in board of education elections," and argued that "the public holds the mayor accountable for the fiscal health of our city and the quality of education for our children. The buck stops here."[75] The October 30 indictment of board member Malcolm George for selling administrative jobs could not have helped public perceptions of the board. Mayor James found himself out of the loop in school policy. Notwithstanding his verbal ruminations about school policy, he was a bystander from day one.

Summary

School reform failed in Newark because the school cartel stayed a step ahead of the politicians. Newark politicians were constantly fighting charges of corruption which kept them off balance. The union leadership in the cartel personalized many of the policy battles, taking the public's attention away from school performance issues. The AIP initiative was a critical battle for the union as it legitimated itself as the defender of teacher rights. The switch to the elected board changed school politics. Although board member Gibson was appointed by the mayor, he was also elected on his own. Nevertheless, he remained convinced that the elected boards were a "bad move for the city." For him the elected board empowers the board employees to "vote up the budget."

"There are 8000 Newark school employees. Although most of the teaching staff do not live in Newark, the 4000 other employees (custodians, cooks, service personnel) do live in the city. They have an interest in higher school budgets. They make a high percentage of voters in school budget elections."[76] The benchmark budget for him was the 1984 budget. At that time the budget was $247 million dollars. In ten years the budget had doubled.

The declining significance of Mayor Gibson in school policy is testimony to the skills of cartel members in confrontational politics. Yatrakis found that Mayor Gibson was not able to live up to his 1971 promises to do something about the functional illiteracy among graduating students.[77] Gibson's own reflections on those years were summarized in this statement, "I never lost interest but I lost the fights." He further stated,

> I have lost three major battles in schools. The fight that was most destructive was the residency issue. Where teachers live does have something to do with the quality of schools. I will always believe that teachers who live outside the city are not concerned with quality. In my childhood teachers lived in Newark and sent their kids to public schools. The first nail in the coffin was the permission to live outside the city.
>
> The second fight was over whether teachers should perform non-teaching functions such as hall monitoring and staffing the playground. Teachers joined unions and now they do not perform any non-teaching duties. It was my appointee (Jesse Jacobs) who cast the deciding vote on professional duties matter. I have made him president of the board. Once you appoint them to the board, you can't tell them what to do. This was the second nail in the coffin. The teachers lived outside the district. None of their children were affected by it. The teachers used their union to get better salary and fringes and preparation as a weapon.
>
> The third fight was over the elected board. The citizens were sold a bill of goods on that issue. If you are told that the mayor makes all appointments and that is not fair, you would probably vote for an elected board. It is interesting that the number of people who voted to approve an elected board far exceed the

> numbers who turn out for school elections. Less than
> 10% vote in school elections. Seven percent of those
> are union members. The board is completely controlled
> by the union. This is the third nail in the coffin.[78]

Conflicts between black mayors and black school board members demonstrate the problems of newcomers assuming political power and making the accommodations necessary to govern. School issues keep appearing on the mayor's agenda when their solutions are outside the reach of the mayor. Therein lies the dilemma for a mayor. If he attempts to address the problems, he runs the risk of alienating the board members. If he ignores or avoids the problems he cannot escape blame for non-action. These recurrent issues in school politics can be among the most frustrating of any mayor's mandate.

In the Gibson case he ran up against a powerful union leader, Carol Graves, who had ties throughout the city and state bureaucracy. She had been able to convince the public that teacher interest was the same as theirs. She had also been able to elect a pliant board. Gibson claims that "Carol Graves is not a bad person. The union just spends all its time fighting for the interest of the teachers, 'If we were better paid, morale would be better.' They opposed any kind of merit system. Everybody gets paid the same. An outstanding teacher can not be given more. There is no incentive to be a teacher outside the love of children."[79]

Former Mayor Gibson concluded that "the mayor cannot control the quality of education unless the school is a department of the city. There is more money in the Newark system than the mayor has to the run the city. The whole system is corrupt. It is completely controlled by political influence."[80] He continued, "The Big Boys complained continually about the schools. They had to have a remedial system to train people."[81] It is that inability to do anything about the schools that makes the mayor's job so difficult when negotiating with unions.

Mayors confront a system that is completely politicized and incapable of making changes. They know that innocent children are being denied an opportunity to invest in their human capital. Gibson came into office a school activist but ended his administration as an isolated bystander. It is true that some of his appointees continued to work for the school system but Gibson never regained the influence he had prior to 1982. His twelve years as player in school policy did not change the way the cartel operated. His successor Mayor James isn't having any better results. The school system retains its reputation as being one of the most corrupt in the nation. Rumors of corruption, illegal activities and mismanagement were finally documented in a huge four-volume 1994 study of the system by the state board of education.[82]

On April 13, 1995 the New Jersey Education Department ordered a takeover of Newark's school district. They cited the incompetence of the school board among several reasons for the takeover. In a fifty-six-page ruling the administrative judge Stephen G. Weiss noted that Newark's spending per pupil was the highest in the state, but only one out of four students passed the High School Proficiency Test. He stated, "That is a description of failure on a very large scale, and if 'abysmal' is too strong a description, it most certainly is distressing to contemplate."[83] Stories about board members' junkets to tropical places and new cars sound very much like the crisis in Detroit when HOPE was able to capture control of the board.[84] Mayor Sharpe James was reportedly "dismayed" but not "surprised" at the state's takeover decision.[85] The Newark board promised to fight the takeover and pressed for a hearing.[86] The state court upheld the takeover and State Education Commissioner Leo Klagholz appointed Dr. Beverly Hall, a Deputy School Chancellor in New York City, acting superintendent for a year. This is clearly a crisis for the Newark public school cartel and may result in the replacement of some board members and the superintendent. However, the total dismembering and replacement of the cartel is as unlikely as is the improvement of student performance in the High School Proficiency. In the *New York Times* article, cartel members were blaming poverty for low test scores. It is a defense that is an insult to the Newark community.

NOTES

1. See Michael Parenti, "Power and Pluralism: A View from the Bottom," *Journal of Politics*, 32, no. 3 (August 1970): 501-532.

2. See Joe Feagin and Harlan Hahn, *Ghetto Revolts* (New York: Macmillan Co., 1973).

3. *Hearings Before United State Commission on Civil Rights*, Newark, New Jersey (September 11-12, 1962), p. 391.

4. Ibid.

5. Joseph Conforti, "The Equity Package: Cities, Families and Schools," *Society* 12 (November/December 1974), p. 26.

6. William Doolittle, "School Board Called a Citadel of Reaction," *Newark Evening News* (January 25, 1967), p. 8.

7. Interview with anonymous source, 1995

8. Carole Martin, "250 Assaults on N.J. Teachers," *Newark Evening Times* (March 30, 1967), p. 1.

9. Gerald Somerville, "Seeking Peace at Vailsburg," *Newark Evening News* (May 9, 1968), p. 1, 13

10. William Doolittle, "Integration Demands," *Newark Evening News* (September 19, 1967), p. 10.

11. Robert Braun, "Support Mounts for Urban School Talk," *The Star-Ledger* (July 21, 1968), p. 1.

12. William Doolittle, "N.J. School Official to Battle Reorganization, Decentralization," *Newark Evening News* (November 13, 1968), p. 27.

13. "Newark School Control by State Seen Unlikely," *Newark Evening News* (April 26, 1968), p. 33.

14. Conforti, op. cit. p. 21.

15. See William Doolittle, " School Takeover Opposed," *Newark Evening News* (June 11, 1968), p. 1, 5.

16. Gerald Pomper, "Ethnic and Group Voting in Nonpartisan Municipal Elections," *Public Opinion Quarterly* 30 (1966): 79-97.

17. Robert Ruth, "Gibson To Consult Teachers Before Board Appointments," *Newark Evening News* (May 24, 1970), p. 5C.

18. Owen Wilkerson, "Gibson Turn His Attention to City's Educational Needs," *Newark Evening News* (June 4, 1970), p. 15.

19. Robert Curvin, "The Persistent Minority: The Black Political Experience in Newark," (Unpublished Dissertation, Princeton University), p. 10.

20. "State of the City Address," Archives of New Jersey Room, Newark Public Library, 1971.

21. Interview with Kenneth Gibson, October 9, 1990.

22. Ibid.

23. See Donald Warshaw, "Victoria Plan Aids Students In Catching Up," *The Star Ledger* (August 15, 1971), p. 39.

24. Charles Q. Finley, "Jacob Attacks Cervase as 'a Liar,'" *The Star Ledger* (February 26, 1971), p. 13.

25. Interview with Kenneth Gibson, op. cit.

26. Ibid.

27. Robert Braun, "Showdown over Newark Schools . . . Again," *The Star Ledger* (November 11, 1971), p. 1B.

28. George Hallam, "Board, Teacher Heading for Clash on Arbitration," *Newark Evening News* (December 6, 1970).

29. Lawrence Hall, "Gibson Challenges Board on 5 Newly-Created Posts," *The Star Ledger* (December 12, 1971), p. 22.

30. Sandra King, "Newark Parents Forced Teacher Transfers," *The Star Ledger*, (October 8, 1972), p. 25.

31. Joshua McMahon, "Vailburg Group, Board Disclose Their Agreement," *The Star Ledger* (March 16, 1973), p. 11.

32. Robert Braun, " Gibson's Education Panel Taking on Critical Tasks," *The Star Ledger* (July 9, 1972), p. 1, 27.

33. Hugh Scott, *The Black School Superintendent: Messiah or Scapegoat* (Washington, D. C. Howard University Press, 1980).

34. See Sandra King, "Staff Shakeup Upsets Head of State Takeover," *The Star Ledger* (October 10, 1975), p. 19.

35. Sandra King, "Schools Auditors Dispel Fear of State Takeover," *The Star Ledger* (January 12, 1976), p. 9.

36. Sandra King, "Burke Sees Success in School Revamp," *The Star Ledger* (December 9, 1976), p. 50.

37. Robert Braun, "Teacher Union Charges Newark Board Misuses Funds," *The Star Ledger* (May 10, 1977), p. 29A.

38. Kenneth Woody, "Gibson Suggests Monitoring of Teachers," *The Star Ledger* (March 30, 1978), p. 38.

39. Robert Braun, "State Orders Burke to Act in Newark School Crisis," *The Star Ledger* (January 11, 1979), p. 1.

40. Robert Braun, "Burke's 'Gap' on Newark: Commissioner, Essex Educators Differ on Progress," *The Star Ledger* (July 1, 1979), p. 47, 50.

41. James Scott, "Planning and Politics in a Black City's Search for School Reform," *Newark: An Assessment* , Stanley Winter, ed. (Newark: New Jersey Institute of Technology, 1978), p. 246.

42. Interview with Kenneth Gibson, op. cit.

43. Katherine Yatrakis, "Electoral Demands and Political Benefits: Minority As Mayority: A Case of Two Mayoral Elections in Newark , N.J.," (Unpublished Ph.D. Dissertation, Columbia University, 1981), pp. 273-274.

44. Barbara Kukla, "Board Ouster Challenged: Grier Cites Gibson Arm-Twisting for Salley," *The Star Ledger* (October 5, 1981), p. 1N.

45. Lawrence H. Hall, "Legal Hitch Forces Newark Board To Confirm School Chief Again," *The Star Ledge*r (September 21, 1981), p. 1, 4.

46. Interview with Columbus Salley, December 11, 1990.

47. Lawrence H. Hall, "Political Controversies Compile a Thick Book at the Board of Education," *The Star Ledger* (May 3, 1982), p. 1N.

48. Patrick Jenkins, "Pupil Truancy Is Slashed by Newark Force," *The Star Ledger* (November 6, 1987) p. 1.

49. Interview with Daniel Gibson, April 7, 1995

50. "Attack on Fiscal Policy Probe," *The Star Ledger* (June 10, 1982), p. 31.

51. Stanley Terrell "Shariff Narrowly Re-elected as Board President: Newark Panel Acts in Holdover Dispute," *Newark Star Ledger* (August 17, 1983), p. 20.

52. Interview with Donald K. Tucker, April 7, 1995.

53. Stanley Terrell, "Newark Board Ousts Its President, Extends Contract for School Chief," *The Star Ledger* (November 8, 1983) p. 1, 9.

54. Stanley Terrell, op. cit. August 17, 1983, p. 20.

55. "PUBS Coalition to Choose School Candidates Tonight," *The Star Ledger* (February 13, 1984), p. 1.

56. Frederick Byrd and Stanley Terrell, "3 Will Be Sure for Seats on Board," *The Star Ledger* (April 12, 1984), p. 1, 16.

57. Frederick Byrd, "Gibson Faults System, Says He can Work with 'Rival' Slate," *The Star Ledger* (April 5, 1984), p. 9.

58. Robert Braun, "Officials Shocked by New Newark Teachers Contract," *The Star Ledger* (August 18, 1985), p. 1, 30.

59. Stanley Terrell, "Newark Board Approves Contract with Teachers," *The Star Ledger* (August 14, 1985), p. 29.

60. Deborah Smith, "Bell: Parents, Teachers, Community Must Join in Improving Education," *New Jersey Afro-American* (August 31, 1985), p. 1, 2.

61. Robert Braun, "Intervention by State Prompts Changes in Newark Teacher Pact," *The Star Ledger* (January 5, 1986), p. 1, 22.

62. Barbara Kukla, "James Makes Bid for Mayor," *The Star Ledger* (February 3, 1986), p. 1N.

63. Edna Bailey, "Four Mayoral Candidates Debate in Newark," *The Star-Ledger* (April 21, 1986), p. 9.

64. "State and Newark Board May Clash on Multi-Year Pact for Schools Chief," *Star Ledger* (October 19, 1986), p. 26.

65. Frederick Byrd, "James Seeks Power to Pick School Board," *Newark Star Ledger* (June 27, 1987), p. 1, 6.

66. Ibid.

67. Frederick Byrd, "Leaders See New Debates With James," *Newark Star Ledger* (June 30, 1987), p. 30.

68. Stanley Terrell, "Newark Board Hears Insistent Plea to Get 'Educational House in Order,'" *The Star Ledger* (July 29, 1987), p. 25.

69. Stanley Terrell, "Fielding Tough Questions: Newark Board Replies to Queries over District's Future," *The Star Ledger* (August 13, 1987), p. 49.

70. Jason Jett, "Newark School Chief Says District Should Get Special Consideration," *The Star Ledger* (September 3, 1987), p. 1.

71. Frederick Byrd," James Requests Referendum on Appointed School Board," *The Star Ledger* (December 19, 1987), p. 1, 17.

72. Frederick Byrd, "School, Business Communities Form Jobs Pact," *The Star Ledger* (May 11, 1987), p. 2N.

73. Angela Stewart, "Panel Created to Improve Newark Education, Head Off Takeover Threat," *The Star Ledger* (October 22, 1987), p. 43.

74. "Newark Schools Face $180 Million Upgrade," *The Star Ledger* (May 20, 1988), p. 33.

75. Frederick Byrd, "James Requests Referendum on Appointed School Board," *The Star Ledger* (November 23, 1988), pp. 1,17.

76. Interview with Daniel Gibson, Jr., April 7, 1995.

77. Yatrakis, op. cit.

78. Interview with Kenneth Gibson, op. cit.

79. Ibid.

80. Ibid.

81. Ibid.

82. See "Comprehensive Compliance Investigation Reports," I-IV, (Trenton: New Jersey State Department of Education, July, 1994).

83. Neil MacFarquhar, "Judge Orders a State Takeover of Newark School District," *New York Times*, (April 14, 1995), p. 1, B6.

84. See Robert Braun, "Klagholz Orders Newark Board to Sell Cars Bought for Members," *The Star Ledger* (January 30, 1995), pp. 1. 10.

85. See Robert Braun, "Klagholz Orders Takeover to 'Liberate' Newark Schools," *The Star Ledger* (May 20, 1995), p. 1, 6.

86. Reginald Roberts, "Newark Board Resolves to Fight State Takeover to the Bitter End," *The Star Ledger* (June 28, 1995), p. 1.

CHAPTER 5

Black Mayors:
Bystanders or Interlopers?

Black mayors have been in office in our nation's largest cities for more than twenty years, but there are now signs that, individually and collectively, they are not any more effective in directing school policy than their white ethnic predecessors. Why did the initial glow of these mayoral stars of the sixties and seventies dim so quickly? Part of the answer can be traced to timing, black mayors came to power when their primary constituency, the black poor, were increasingly bored, disillusioned, and apathetic. Undoubtedly frustrated by not being able to improve their life chances, inner city residents complain about the poor quality of city schools, street crime, decaying infrastructure, and the slow rate of economic redevelopment. They don't like the situation any more than their white critics do. In our public school systems, the quality of schools sank dramatically after the sixties. More importantly, the plight of the black poor has not changed after years of anti-poverty programs and friendly hearings in City Hall. During their tenures, Gibson, Hatcher, and Young were all accused of becoming the new apologists for the status quo.

City Hall and Schools

In the early days of the nation's history, a tradition of keeping the mayor out of school politics was established. The state legislators and independent school boards worked diligently to keep city mayors as bystanders in education affairs. Their efforts have been only partially successful. The history of big city schools indicates that mayors have always been very involved in the evolution and development of public schools. Would school policy be better served by more involvement of mayors? Russell Murphy, the political scientist, concluded that the notion of strong mayoral powers has never been accepted as a necessary condition for democracy in cities. According to Murphy, early American, governing elites also distrusted the electorate's judgment regarding any matters which they felt were crucial to the new Republic's future.[1] Hence they sought to lodge public education between the margins of state and local community control. As mayors' roles changed and they began to emerge with increased power and become more than just ceremonial heads of local government, they grew more involved in educational policy.

Today the mayor is expected to address educational problems and needs. Mayors are required to have opinions about a wide range of social problems, including schools. Controversy arises when the mayor attempts to intervene directly in school policy. The barrier that was erected to protect schools from politics often denies Board of Education members mayoral political protection. Mayor Young contended that "schools suffer because of its (not being a part of the mayor's responsibility)."[2]

The election of black mayors introduced an added challenge to the cartel's monopoly on school policy. Although their election did not result demands for charter revisions and more mayor-appointed boards, black mayors were initially thought to be the Robespierre(s) of city politics. Hindsight tells us that the election of a black mayor was a harbinger of a predominantly black city. Twenty years ago, these mayors were expected to help to alleviate the misery of the poor, halt the ugliness of the downtown retail sectors, and stop the public schools from graduating functional illiterates. Kenneth Gibson was elected in 1970; Richard Hatcher in 1967, and Coleman Young in 1973. Each represented the first of their race to be elected mayor in their city. Their elections created high expectations.

The appointment of a black superintendent of schools in Newark (1973), Detroit (1975) and Gary (1980) represented significant breakthroughs in the rise of black political power. At last black voters had political control of two major units of urban governance, the superintendency and the mayoralty. But what were vehicles for city hall/superintendent office coordination? Could these two leaders work together effectively? In each city blacks were elected president of school boards before a black man was elected mayor. The election of a black president of the board suggests a readiness within the local education community to elect blacks for visible leadership positions. This history supports the findings of Robert Dahl's review of the school community, which yielded three propositions.

> First, the number of citizens who participate directly in important decisions bearing on the public school is small. . . . Second, direct influence over decisions in public education seems to be exerted almost entirely by public officials. Third, in recent years the chief center of direct influence has been the mayor and his appointees on the Board of Education, rather than the superintendent.[3]

In 1970 Leigh Stelzer conducted a nationwide study of school boards and found little difference in the social composition of school board members, regardless of their selection process. He concluded that "the most striking difference between members of elective and appointive boards is the extent to which the appointive boards are engaged in what can only be described as a network of educational associations. Appointive members are more likely to have participated in education-related activities prior to their board service."[4] In Gary most appointees were members of the school activist community prior to their appointments. Gary elected to switch to an elected board after Hatcher left office. Nevertheless, former Mayor Hatcher remains opposed to an elected board.

> I did not agree with the idea of going with an elected school board. When you have a single appointing source, you can vote against the mayor. Now it is just who is the best politician? The five people elected are the best politicians. They are not the best five board members to make policy judgment. The appointment process gave us the best people. All you have done with

> an elected board is create another city council to run
> the schools. They have to worry about whether they
> are going to be reelected. There is less focus on schools
> and less focus on efficiency.[5]

Hatcher claims that Gary schools were very inefficient when contracting out decisions. They hired outsiders when services were available in the community. He also claims that factions developed in an elected board. He believed that mayors would restrain them from interfering in school affairs. "I followed a self-imposed restraint on school matters. I left it up to the board. I did not interfere with the operation of the schools."[6] Coleman Young used the same disclaimer:[7] John Elliot, head of the DFT, confirmed the mayor's disclaimer

> I never saw any role for the mayor but a passing or
> supporting role. I never talk to the Mayor at a fund
> raiser or church dinner. Alonzo Bates never said the
> Mayor wants this. . . . I never had a school related
> conversation with Mayor (since he has been mayor).
> The way I know what he wants is when he is
> interviewed. He make noises about the school system
> (like in Chicago and New York) but he has never done
> anything about it that I am aware of. I never felt the
> Mayor was trying to impose his will on the school system.[8]

Given the history of mayoral involvement in school politics and policies, it was inevitable that the black constituency would expect their mayors to be active in school politics. However, it was less clear how success in municipal politics would translate effectively into school politics. There have been adjustment problems for both the school community and the new black occupants of city hall.

School Politics and City Politics

Because the school activist community was recruited from the same pool as the municipal politicians, one would assume that cooperation between them would be easier. As earlier case studies demonstrated, this was not always the case. School politicians may become as highly visible as other elected officials and thus amass political clout that rivals the other elected leaders. School politicians often had to bargain with municipal officials over policy which overlapped their respective domains.

Regardless of the legal structure of school governance, mayors traditionally have performed the following functions: electoral (participation directly and indirectly in school elections), public safety (providing police protection for schools, students, and personnel), mediation (offering their good offices for dispute settlements between unions and the school board) and financial (supporting millage elections and lobbying for state aid). These functions are routine and part of the unwritten mayoral job description. Unfortunately, mayors get little visibility or credit for doing these jobs well; the emotion-laden conflicts that accompany the mayor's intervention in school policies incite the school activist community to protect their turf.

Robert Salisbury argued that "autonomous schools may be unresponsive to important groups in the community whose interests are not effectively served by the dominant values of professional schoolmen."[9] He endorsed the direct involvement of Mayor Richard Daley in school administration for the sake of racial integration. Salisbury, like many others, believed that integration would remain a public policy issue, and weak mayoral control was not the best way to implement it. Paul Peterson's (1985) later work concerning Chicago schools contended that Mayor Richard Daley had all the influence he needed with the school board. Peterson concluded that Daley was a pluralist bargainer and compromiser who sought to maximize his influence in school policy by persuasion.[10]

Scholars have analyzed the role of mayors by investigating the response of schools to court-ordered desegregation decrees.[11] Detroit Superintendent Jefferson admitted that Coleman Young was involved in trying to implement the 1976 court ruling to integrate Detroit schools. According to Jefferson, the Mayor did not want Detroit busing to degenerate into a racial conflict as it did in Boston. The new mayor saw his role as protecting the public safety.[12] Coleman Young was not hesitant to advocate incorporating the administration of the school system into a city department. During the 1987 teacher strike the mayor restated his position. Although he denied that he was "campaigning to run the schools" he thought the current method of running schools was ineffective and should be replaced by a system more accountable to city control.[13] This, of course, brought a quick response from the board vice president Mary Blackmon.

> This board is very responsive. . . . We are directly accountable to the people by whom we were elected. If they are not satisfied, there is a (recall) process to deal with that.
>
> I don't think any outside source has any right to determine the board's accountability. I know of no more dedicated group of elected official than the people on this board. As a practical matter, we are full-time officials who work without compensation. We give 30, 35, 40, hours a week of our time fighting hard to provide educational quality for young people.[14]

Three days later *The Detroit News* ran an editorial condemning the board's handling of the teacher strike but expressing reservations about Young's proposal to have the schools under city control. The editorial reported the record of big city mayors and school administration as "mixed."[15] Nevertheless, Young comments that people "would know where to go when they look for somebody to blame"[16] is consistent with views held by Jerome Zeigler, a former mayoral aide. He suggested that "more than any other elected official, the mayor must live with the overall consequences of school performance."[17]

Dunaway claims that mayors play both visible and invisible roles in the making of school policies. Visible roles include: appointing, decision-making, public statement-making, and the coordinating and providing of services. The invisible roles include consultation with the school board over the appointment of administrators, party brokering, background discussions with activists and the media, and providing school planners with data. Zeigler cites four reasons why the traditional separation between City Hall and the board of education is breaking down. " (1) citizen concern over the quality of public schools; (2) growing interaction between the school system and other departments and agencies of city government; (3) the interrelationship of the educational system with other city problems and conditions facing the mayor; and (4) intervention by the federal government in local school affairs through the courts or federal social and educational programs."[18]

Some elected mayors have taken a high profile in school politics with mixed results. Coleman Young's endorsement of school board members in the 1989 election did not help much. Mayor Martin Katz , Richard Hatcher's predecessor, once suggested that the entire Gary school board, appointed by him, should resign if it couldn't work out a balance between its role and that of the superintendent. They didn't resign and continued their feud.

Throughout the history of the cities in our study, white mayors have been more involved than their black counterparts in school policy. Detroit Mayor James Couzen blocked the appointment of Randall Condon to the superintendency of schools. Mayor Katz of Gary publicly advocated removing his appointees from the school board after their actions threatened the accreditation of the school system. Throughout the history of the three systems studied, there are few instances in which school board-appointed superintendents were political enemies of the incumbents. Newark Mayor Hugh Addonizio, Gibson's predecessor, was "a pivotal and formidable factor in school affairs."[19] He promoted an expansion of the system and was the first to advocate the election of board members. It was clear during his administration that education was a "political function." No black council members challenged Addonizio's control over board affairs.[20]

History has shown that mayors can exert influence in school politics. Are black mayors expected to do otherwise? Black mayors are newcomers to school politics, and many are reluctant to enter the political domain of school politicians. The three case studies suggest that if they entered the school board, they were considered interlopers. Gibson got into trouble trying to remove one of his appointees. Simply put, black mayors did not have much impact on school policy. Why? The inhibitory element may be related to the fact that black mayors gained power when the black middle class was attempting to consolidate its hold on power in the school cartel. Deferring to insiders' preference is not uncommon for new mayors who seek reciprocity from other elected officials. Arthur Jefferson allowed that "Coleman Young didn't say anything publicly in 1975 (the year of his appointment). He respected our independence."[21] The new superintendent did not interact with the mayor until after the court ordered Detroit schools to desegregate. Jefferson then met with the police chief and the mayor made members of his staff available. Desegregation was a public safety issue.

Mayor Young recognized the limitations of his position. Nevertheless, this did not prevent him from commenting on school reform schemes such as the Detroit Compact, i.e., a joint business/ school improvement effort. In an interview with Marion Orr, a political scientist, Young stated "The mayor can't do a damn thing in education. I try to support it all I can. But I try to stay out of things I can't control."[22] Perhaps the mayor protested too much, as he does not hesitate to voice an opinion if school policy overlaps with city politics. He is particularly concerned about residency requirements.

> I think the mayor should be responsible for education. Now there are two separate forms of government. These are conflicting forms of government. I would urge residency. Our residency requirement does not apply to teachers. I would make waivers in the case of specialists. Middle class blacks are leaving the city. They send their children to schools outside the city. A nonresidency relieves them of a degree of responsibility to make the various efforts to assure quality education. Those who draw salaries in the city should pay taxes.[23]

The mayor knew that if middle-class blacks left, the city's treasury would be hurt, because they would not be paying the city income tax rate. The loss of middle-class residents could also depreciate property values. Teachers should be expected to live near their students and be a part of the community. If city schools are not good enough for the children of teachers and administrators, then city residents should be alarmed that other children are forced to attend these schools. The promise of new linkage between the schools and economic planning is yet to be realized.

School Policy Overlaps?

The dreadful financial condition of public schools followed the economic decline of their host cities. Rust-Belt cities were caught in a Catch-22 situation. In order to create good schools, they need a stable economy. Without a stable economy, it is difficult to maintain good schools. Inadequate schools create weak entry level labor market candidates. A city with poorly trained workers finds it nearly impossible to attract new investors. It follows that educators and City Hall should closely coordinate their activities or at least agree on long-term goals. Unfortunately, in the cities in this study, policies don't overlap so much as they run parallel. The opportunities for policy intersection are not there.

Black mayors did not inherit *tabula rasa* cities. In fact, they came to power when jobs and people were leaving the city. To complicate matters, the tax base declined at a time when more money was needed to fund schools. School bureaucracies, already entrenched, expanded their missions to include more social services. Teacher unions, relatively weak under their white predecessors, became a mighty force in city politics. The recovery policies of black mayors have delayed, not reversed, economic conditions. Yet many local newspapers implied that black mayors have made things worse. The facts do not support such contentions.

City Life and Nostalgia

Perhaps the most disturbing aspect of the criticisms of black elected officials is the unfettered nostalgia for the white liberal era by otherwise sober urban observers. Journalists seem particularly prone to exaggerate the achievements of the past. Readers are led to believe that the stewardship of white mayors occurred in periods of élan. They contend that white mayors could contain and quarantine crime in the poor white and "Negro section" of town, while the new black mayors have not prevented criminals from penetrating the city's "best" neighborhoods.

According to this revisionist account, the old regime maintained a city where there was no newsworthy graft, nepotism, or corruption. Budgets were balanced routinely, and the surpluses often embarrassed the mayor and city councils. Of course, taxes were always kept low. No one boarded up homes, because when families moved out, their homes were sold to new families. More important, city residents could send their children to public schools where they consistently received an excellent education. Everyone was reading at their grade levels and school dropouts were rare. The SAT scores were off the scale. This version of the 1950s and '60s represents the mythical city of suburbanites. Journalists have reified this vision of the old city by focusing on the great and happy moments of the city's history. Unfortunately, however, the historical data do not support this one-sided vision. Although many of these claims have been repeatedly debunked by urban historians, purveyors of this myth persist in lamenting the loss of this city. How could black mayors as a group measure up to the political good times after World War II? There is always a tendency to romanticize the past, but the general public seems to lean on the myth for psychological support. It is reasonable to assume that the attack against cities serves another purpose.

The relentlessly negative critiques of black mayors by former residents is a part of a psychological need to disassociate themselves from the current residents of the city. It has allowed those who have fled to engage in what Ken Kenitson calls "cosmic alienation," a sense of being unceremoniously forced out of the city.[24] For example, suburban residents of Detroit are among the harshest critics of former mayor Coleman Young. "Young-bashing" was a favorite pastime among former city residents. They blamed him for all of the ills of the city. There are still people who believe that Hatcher's anti-corporate rhetoric was one of the causes of the decline of the U.S. Steel in Gary.

Even before Gibson's second term, critics were complaining about the lack of miracles. Newark's Gibson, according to Willa Johnson, was selected because of his "quiet and unobtrusive" manner. Trained as an engineer, Gibson made education part of his campaign for the office, yet he could not persuade the school bureaucracy to focus its resources on teaching reading skills. Johnson attributes Gibson's initial failure to achieve change to institutional arrangements which inhibit all black mayors from acting.

> The election of a Black man to political office is somewhat similar to substituting a new pitcher in a baseball game. The pitcher may have a playing style which is quite different from that of the other players, but he does not change the rules of the game. If he changes the rules, he is thrown out of the contest.[25]

The plight of black mayors is not just a commentary on the woes of blacks in political office, or on the conflictual nature of urban management, but rather on the governing difficulties experienced by these mayors under conditions of economic disinvestment. The failure of direct action to solve problems raises serious questions about the viability of central city economies in a postindustrial society. Can an urban nation leave the responsibility of housing and feeding of the poor solely to the elected officials of the central cities? Despite claims that an entirely urban-based economy can be built around welfare benefits and government redistribution programs, the economies of cities have been allowed to stagnate.

Equally disturbing is the impact of the slow- or no-growth economy on the attitudes of black youths. Many young people have become disillusioned about their life chances and view politicians as irrelevant to their future. Having been born after the turbulent years of the late 1960s, most black youths are unaware of the struggles to elect black mayors. It has been difficult to convince the youth that cities have changed radically under the stewardship of black mayors and school board members.

The political clock of youth runs out faster than that of their elders. They see their future as a tunnel of powerlessness. This perception has contributed to nihilism, self-abuse, and political alienation in these three inner cities. Yet some black politicians see hope in the election of the new generation of black mayors.

Kurt L. Schmoke, Mayor of Baltimore and former Rhodes Scholar, asserted the following in an interview: "The first generation mayors were pioneers. . . . For the first generation, it was a leap of faith that they could be mayor. The second generation is closer to conventional urban politicians."[26] Linda Williams, a political scientist, is also optimistic but for different reasons. She states, "The new breed of black mayors tends to be different in terms of their focus on city-wide development efforts as opposed to even running on a banner of changes for minority and poor communities. . . . New Black mayors have consciously shaped their image so as not to be threatening to middle-class blacks or to white America."[27] Wilkins places his faith in the emergence and acceptance of black technocrats. Williams suggests that a city-wide approach will lead to more coalition politics, which will displace racial politics. Robert Gurwitt made a similar generational replacement, coalition-building argument after the 1989 elections. Neither Wilkins nor Williams seems to be arguing that embracing non-racial issues will make the mayor's race irrelevant.

Why should black residents elect another black mayor? Aside from the symbolic significance and the ethnic secession argument, the assumption that black mayors understand the complexity of black culture and, hence, are most qualified to deal with the causes of crime and unemployment, is a syllogism. The culture of the ghetto (to use a more modern term, the underclass) is an ever-changing one with nuances that make the experiential knowledge held by ethnically and upwardly mobile cohorts outdated. It may be that newly elected black mayors, with first generation middle-class credentials, can add little to the solving of urban problems. Their elections may have inflated their real influence in policy making, particularly school policy.

People see black elected officials "in power," and it changes their notion of their relationship to power. However, it is often purely a vicarious experience. White society is not always forced to deal with and listen to blacks once they assume the power of local government. As the work of Clarence Stone on Atlanta has suggested, whites do cooperate with black elected officials for the interest of social production.[28] In our three cities whites abandoned membership in the cartels when blacks become the majority. But as our study suggested, the ghosts of the white predecessors were clearly present in the deliberations of the black successors.

Given the history of the country (i.e., the isolation of blacks from whites), it is inevitable that these groups may have different views about the uses of power. Some white board members concluded that blacks wanted power for social reasons, and that they wanted power as a way to participate in the management of the schools. Many whites perceive that blacks feel psychologically left out and deprived of power. This is the message many whites hear in the rhetoric of black politicians. For their own reasons, whites, as grantors of power, assume altruism in the motives of individual black politicians. The early black mayors such as Richard Hatcher felt that power was an instrument of social uplift for their black constituency and a statement of their personal achievement. Many black mayors saw their election as the beginning of a real power redistribution. This view of power proved to be a mirage.

In other words, the preemptive power of economic elites makes the plotting of new and variant policies of black mayors difficult, if not impossible. The economic elite bring so much clout to the bargaining table that their preferences dominate the discussions. The general point about entrenched interests is also supported by the work of Clarence Stone. He introduced the term "preemptive power," which he defines as "power as a capacity to occupy, hold, and make use of a strategic position."[29] The economic elites are able to protect their interests with regularity because of their position in the governing process. In fact little can be done without them. This lesson was learned by Kenneth Gibson and Coleman Young in their first terms. Stone observes that "white business interest and black officeholders have evolved a system of reciprocal benefit, which each has a strong incentive to protect. They are thus willing to combine their resources in exercising together the community's leadership role."[30]

Different public policy issues have different configurations of support and opposition. According to Persons, a black mayor's leverage stems from his perceived or real support in the black community, particularly from middle-class blacks.[31] Without that support he is weakened in racially divisive issues when confronted with strong white opposition. In non-racial issues, the mayor is virtually powerless when faced with unified opposition. The trick for black mayors is to create the perception among the middle-class constituency that their interests are at stake. Detroit does not have a large white-collar middle class. Yet Coleman Young has been successful in leveraging the support of the working class community, which has been the mainstay of his political power. Heavily organized by the United Auto Workers (UAW), the working class has supported the mayor and his downtown development projects. The unionists have not attempted to confront the entrenched interests, but rather they have supported automobile companies.

It is clear that the white business communities in Newark and Detroit have survived after the election of black mayors. With the onset of the post-industrial economy, and concomitant internationalization of labor and production, will the function of cities and their leaders change? The early signs suggest that black mayors are adaptable. Could the new generation of black leaders— e.g. Thomas Barnes (Gary), Sharpe James (Newark), and Dennis Archer (Detroit)—do a better job of leading their city in this transition? Presumably, new leaders would not be bound by the old notions of the city—they could start fresh.

Relying on this assumption, the electorate in Gary and Newark terminated the careers of their mayors, Richard Hatcher and Kenneth Gibson. Young retired after 20 years in office. The voters of these cities replaced three men who were considered national authorities in urban governance with lesser-known local politicians. Hatcher and Gibson were not able to offset the erosive effects of the city's socio-economic context of their tenure nor cogently to articulate their visions of a New Gary and a New Newark.

The plight of black mayors may be characterized as a by-product of unappreciated and unanticipated offsetting events. Few analysts predicted the erosive effects of these forces during the rise of black mayors. These juxtapositions include: white media/

black administration; anti-political machine sentiments/extra-government institutional needs; the availability of economic leveraging grants-in-aids/absence of indigenous developers; and the instability of residential households/need for internal stable tax base. The mechanisms needed for creating a coalition of these forces are beyond the control of black mayors. The convergence of these forces and those of the governing needs of the black mayors is unlikely. A brief discussion of these forces suggests the reasons behind the continued parallels of these forces.

White Media, Black Politicians

Jeffrey Pressman's essay on the requirements of mayoral leadership questioned the possibility of this leadership in cities in which the media were not favorable and supportive.[32] In most black-led cities, the newspapers have been reluctant, if not hostile, partners in promoting city policy. Small independent black-owned weeklies have not enjoyed an increase in status or readership as a result of the election of black mayors. The resources of the larger white dailies offset the circulation of black weeklies. Besides, few whites read black newspapers. Although many whites have abandoned the city for the suburbs, they regard the dailies as their link to the central city.

When television evening news features city politics if is often done in headline style. Rarely are the names and activities of suburban government officials mentioned in the twenty-minute presentations of talking heads, moving emergency vehicles, and light banter that characterize local news. In this era of fast-food tabloid-type news reporting, any in-depth account of anything takes too long. Print and broadcast media not only report and interpret the news, they often set the agenda (e.g., a feature story on the dangers of guns in schools could trigger a major debate about civil liberties). Black mayors were elected in an era when broadcast news, particularly television, had eclipsed its print counterparts as the source of news for younger viewers. Many large city dailies have lost some of their influence in city politics, and most are no longer locally owned. Most are part of large newspaper chains (e.g., Gannett and Knight-Ridder) are partners in a joint operating agreement. *The Detroit Free Press* and the *Detroit News* operate under such an agreement.

In spite of new technology and lower operating costs, newspapers have not stopped the erosion of their influence. Black mayors are not dealing with publishers who are also community leaders. They are mobile employees seeking to impress an absentee owner. Craig T. Ladwig, a former editor for Knight-Ridder newspapers, reached a similar conclusion in an editorial after the recent announcement of the merger of the two Detroit papers. The JOA had been approved by the U.S. Supreme Court. He believed readers would turn away from these types of corporate journalism. Real journalism for him is indigenous ownership: "It is a man or woman on the premises who owns controlling interest in the press. It is an owner, however irritating to the various political ambitions about town, who can be depended upon to act on conviction rather than posture in exercising both editorial voice and news judgment."[33]

In a strange twist, the local television anchors have become the stars of the media. Male anchors enjoy as much name recognition as the mayor. Although these individuals may be recent arrivals to the city and know little about the city's political history, their views are respected by the public. They are free to challenge city officials and their policies. In Detroit, when the leading anchor person is thought to be having a feud with the mayor, such disagreements are significant. In addition, black mayors have found that the traditional weekly news briefing is a poor vehicle for dominating the evening news. Reporters seem interested only in sound bites and quotable materials, not long-winded explanations of city policies. In this post-Watergate era, they are less interested in the details of policy. It's not just that reporters resist this information; rather, they do not want to be scooped on scandals and misdeeds. For most reporters the primary criterion of a story is its audience appeal: Will the story appeal to our white suburban viewers and readers? The more critical the stories, the more credibility they assume among readers. Too many good news stories about the cities may not attract viewers or sell newspapers. Viewers tend to be more interested in the woes of urban life.

In defense of the publishers and station owners, reporters claim that they are in business to make a profit. The nature of the ratings game and newspaper subscription sales make sensationalism inevitable. They print what people want to read and broadcast what people want to see and hear. Like their national counterparts city reporters regard their role as adversarial—ferreting out the misdeeds of politicians. Black mayors and school board members should not expect sympathetic treatment from the media, but many do. Some black mayors believe that highly personalized treatment of city politics plays into the hands of the racists by focusing on mismanagement, crime, and corruption. Others claim the local coverage focuses on the private lives of black mayors and school board members at the expense of public discourse on public policy.

Journalists often abuse their access to power. In a few cases they become the news. In slow news periods they are not averse to fishing for personal items. In the old days a mayor could call the editor and tone down sensitive materials. Modern editors are less likely to kill stories for politicians if the reporter's sources can be verified. The public seems to want more of this type of sensationalist coverage. Because of intense competition for news there is a disinclination to print news releases from the mayor's press secretary. Every reporter is looking for a scoop.

The Marasmus of Political Machines

Perhaps the legacy of black stewardship in cities will be the total dismantling of local political machines. The decline of the local political party patronage came at the time when black politicians were freshmen in city hall. The erosion of political parties started with the invention of the civil service employee unions in the sixties and consolidated with the U.S. Supreme Court decision against arbitrary patronage dismissal (*Elrod v. Burns*, 1976).[34] The old patronage system is gone. There are few ways of rewarding working-class people for participation in politics. Urban politics has become a middle-class activity performed for the uplift of the poor. The same can be said for school policy. Alonzo Bates, a Detroit former board member and chair of the personnel committee, saw his role as expanding opportunities for blacks. He recalled "our role was more than just to educate but to give blacks positions and jobs, so that they can hire other blacks in the future."[35] He was very proud of his role in steering contracts to black vendors under the board EEOC policy.

In this study black mayors did not maintain or nurture political organizations. This fact does not preclude them from behaving as if they are controlling a political organization. They have not challenged journalists' characterizations of a political machine after landslide reelections. Yet none have devoted time building the infrastructure or creating the preconditions for the development of an effective organization. An effective political organization for black mayors would include full-time representation at the precinct levels in city politics; ideological cohorts in the leadership of supportive community organizations; mechanisms for mobilizing the electorate (e.g., campaign facilities and transportation); an extensive communication network capable of providing reliable and continual contact with members of the network; a queuing and training system for new recruits; and a reliable sanctioning and purging system.

No black mayor in this study can claim such an organization. Coleman Young, one of the nation's longest serving mayors, did not have an organization that met these requirements.[36] He relied primarily on personal IOUs, political advertising, and his record for reelection. The defeats of Mayors Kenneth Gibson and Richard Hatcher have been traced to personal misjudgments and administrative problems within their administrations, not to any collapse of their political organizations. In other words, black mayors of large cities have not continued political machines left by their white predecessors or established new ones. Black mayors like Gibson ran against the political machine, arguing it is nefarious to black interests. The three mayors in this study saw themselves as reformers.

The absence of organized recruiting and training mechanisms, i.e., a strong political organization, creates uncertainties about the future leadership. These mayors seems to be suffering from the "Prince of Wales Effect." That is, they will not prepare for leadership succession for fear of facilitating it. Unlike their white counterparts, black officials do not have big law firm jobs waiting. Many consider their job a last stop before retirement.

The flight from institutionalizing political power is consistent with the adhocracy practiced by black mayors. This reliance on political improvising promotes the personalization of politics. The political insecurity of black mayors is exemplified by their seeming preference for loyalty over expertise. In Coleman Young's first term some new black administrators had to learn administration while leading a city agency. The administrators rely heavily on civil servants and are evaluated only if there is a scandal of some kind. Otherwise, City Hall leaves them alone.

Elected officials create personalized reelection groups rather than coordinate party organizations. Jerry Hagstrom believes mayoral campaigns have gone the route of presidential elections. The campaigns are increasingly media oriented with a full array of campaign advertisements and themes. Hagstrom anticipates danger in this trend.

> As candidates have become more dependent on TV and radio ads and direct-mail appeals, campaign costs have skyrocketed. Because most of the campaign money is raised from firms and individuals that do business with the cities, questions of conflict of interest and political favoritism are arising. Ethical questions have been raised particularly about campaign contributions from real estate interest, as growth has become a controversial campaign issue in many communities.[37]

Without a clearly defined constituency or an organizational reference group (particularly if they play a major role in the reelection campaign), the mayor's staff becomes more isolated from street-level politics. Since their power is derived from association with the mayor rather than any constituency, they become sycophants at the expense of providing the mayor with objective advice. The shift to media-oriented campaigns also hurts the mayor. Operating without a between-elections organization, mayors increasingly see themselves as independent actors fighting for survival.

The Scarcity of Indigenous Developers

Revitalizing a city like Gary, Indiana, requires capital for investment. If such capital is not forthcoming from the federal government, then it must be obtained locally. Republican presidents have been unwilling to fund the projects of developers and urban Democratic elected officials. The State of Indiana has not stepped in to restore its most industrial city to health. This withdrawal of federal support has truncated the development of the pro-growth coalition.[38] If there is a global flow of capital, then the Garys and the Detroits are competing with Mexico and Taiwan as well as with U.S. Sun-Belt cities.

If there is widespread disinvestment in old Rust-Belt cities like those in the three case studies, then where is the capital to come from? Some political economists have concluded that the resources needed are so vast that only the federal government can provide capital necessary to rehabilitate old cities.[39] We should concentrate on the new cities and ignore the old ones. This strategy would necessitate a national industrial policy and diversion of funds now going to other parts of the economy.

For black mayors, talk of global flow of capital and disinvestment sounds interesting, but it does not solve their immediate problem—how to build or rebuild the city's economy in the face of competing cities and changing technologies. Their white predecessors never had to worry about Japanese industries taking away American jobs. Who would have predicted that the invention of communication satellites would enable credit card companies to beam clerical work to third-world nations to save labor costs?

White mayors of the 1950s also did not have to contend with local banks discriminating against homeowners and businessmen. In Detroit there are black entrepreneurs (fast food franchise owners) with assets of more than five million dollars who complain about having to go outside the state to raise capital. Despite the success of these individuals, none of them alone or in combination with other black entrepreneurs could raise enough capital to sponsor a major rehabilitation of the city downtown retail area. Accordingly, black entrepreneurs were not the beneficiaries of Urban Development Action Grants (UDAG). They did not have the leveraging capital to utilize these grants.

The Fiscal Crisis of Rust-Belt Households

Increasingly, the cities in this study are havens for the poor and working poor. A decade ago Detroit was one of thirteen cities described as having 20% or more of its population in poverty. The data show a persistence of poverty.[40] These individuals are least able to pay property, income, or sales taxes. These groups are also over-represented among single-parent families. Yet they have been sharing the burden of financing the state budget with those who live in the suburbs and make more money. They often have to pay higher auto insurance rates and transportation to retail markets in the suburbs. The non-resident municipal income tax, thought to be a way to collect taxes from a peripatetic middle class, has failed as a revenue-generating policy, as many companies and retail businesses have moved their locations to the suburbs. In addition, the central cities are stuck with a disproportionate amount of untaxable properties (e.g., state office buildings, universities, and museums).

As we will discuss in chapter seven , the collapse and downsizing of some manufacturing industries has left old cities with an unemployed and unemployable labor force. Young people of Gary and Detroit cannot expect to follow their parents into the steel mills and automobile plants. Unfit for the post-industrial economy, the poor seem not to be protesting their lack of work but rather to be acquiescing.

Constituency Disengagement

Municipal elections take on different meanings in every election. School elections are even more difficult to read.

Determining who wins and who loses is just part of the meaning of elections. It has been argued elsewhere that "politicians like elections because, through them, their mandates can be legitimated, voters like them because they empower the citizen, and parties welcome them because they energize their political organizations."[41] Black mayors have special problems, since they were swept into power by mobilizing unusual numbers of weak Democratic voters. In our three cities the first election of a black mayor is seen by black voters as obligatory: "We must vote to elect the first black mayor and make history." Voting is viewed as tantamount to joining the movement. Voter turnout is high. Victory is celebrated collectively. Indeed, this brief interregnum before and after the election may be seen as the peak mobilization period. The glow of being in power for first-termers is filled with symbolism and celebrations.

The onset of declining constituency interest starts before the end of the first term. First-term mayors can usually argue for and campaign on the issue of "give us more time." They can claim that a second term will bring fundamental changes in the way things are done in City Hall. Maintaining constituency interest is aided by intense media coverage and continual campaigning by the new mayors. The chance for reelection is very high, but there is usually a lower turnout.

The second term offers the mayor a second chance to demonstrate management and governing skills. Many of the simple mistakes of the first term are corrected. Yet a malaise sets in as economic conditions continue to deteriorate. The announced big redevelopment project provides some relief, but construction projects take a long time. Residents see little if any improvement in their respective neighborhoods.

The third term is characterized by the collapse of the original mobilized group. They may still support the mayor but they do not vote. They have either lost interest in electoral politics or are convinced that the mayor can win reelection easily. The novelty of electing a black mayor has worn off. If the mayor has a weak opponent, then reelection is relatively assured. If the opponent is competitive, the mayor can be defeated. To avoid low turnouts, mayors may exaggerate the chances of his opponents or manipulate issues to create uncertainty among his original constituency. Only Coleman Young was able to survive defeat.

Constituency disengagement is not limited to black mayors. School elections in Gary and Newark have experienced a falloff in turnout after the initial referendum to switch from the appointed board to an elected one. Detroit elections also have seen ups and downs in turnouts. Recall that the 1988 Detroit election generated considerable interest but little change in the turnout percentage among voters.

Given the problems of offsetting parallels discussed earlier and the possibility of constituency disengagement, the question of the performance of black mayors and school boards must be considered in contextual terms. Single case studies are the only way to discern the ills of a particular mayor or why a seemingly ineffective board member keeps getting elected. It is difficult to compare the mayors in this study, who are by-products of a post-industrial society, with their white predecessors. They must be seen within the context of the idiosyncratic politics of their city.

Summary

School politics have transformed the mayor into an interloper in education in the three case studies in this book. At first glance it appears that black mayors were less powerful than their white counterparts. A closer look reveals that black mayors came to City Hall after the first stage of black involvement (i.e., access and recognition period) in school policies. White mayors held office when there were virtually no black administrators, few black teachers, and when the student population was being slowly transformed into a black majority. De facto segregation was the norm. Local civil rights leaders included public schools on their protest agenda. Accordingly, black protesters were fighting the white establishment. When blacks took over City Hall, it was difficult to rally people against the black establishment.

In the second stage (i.e. competition and confrontation) blacks had black candidates for mayors as allies against the all white school cartel. Black mayors and superintendent became the norm in this stage. The school cartel had to adapt to racial changes in the voting population. Blacks members of the cartel readily accepted the ideology and rules of the coalition.

The third stage of black involvement (consolidation and routinization of power) pitted black mayors against the interest of the cartel. This explains why Gary and Newark went to the elected school board. Indeed blacks became strong advocates of politically independent school boards. Black mayors lost whatever influence they had in the cartel. As we reach the current stage, we see that the school is in fiscal crisis, but the cartel's power is still in tact. The prospects for increased mayoral influence is guarded. Black mayors cannot expect black heads of teacher unions to lessen demands for pay increases in order to keep property taxes low. It is unlikely that black mayors could convince the public that the return to the appointed board will save the schools. Coleman Young, perhaps the strongest of the black mayors we studied, could not convince the public that change was necessary. The weakness of the inner city mayors in school policy has created a vacuum which allows governors to become spokesmen on educational issues. We will discuss later why mayors and governors are now considered rivals in the education improvement arena.

The disinclination either to nurture extant political organizations or to create new ones may be related to the skewed racial polarization in cities with black mayors. Former Mayor Richard Hatcher had a well-organized volunteer group, but it degenerated over his twenty-year tenure. Middle-class black professionals simply moved away from the city. The government shrank as the population declined. Hatcher never enjoyed the patronage of his white predecessors. Few still have mini-ethnic machines actively competing to prove to the city their control of districts or voting turnout. The organizational base of black mayors is so weak that teacher unions have emerged as a force in non-board elections.

If there is a real structural impediment to blacks ever creating an economic base in central cities comparable to their suburban counterparts, it is the lack of indigenous developers. There is no single minority individual with the capital to develop the riverfronts of Gary and Detroit. Most black mayors have to push to include minority contractors as subcontractors in city projects. The recent U.S. Supreme Court decision in the Richmond Case (i.e. outlawing racial set-asides) makes that effort more difficult, if not impossible.

Finally, many black mayors have gained prominence because they were the first members of their race to lead the city. When that novelty wears off, many find themselves saying grace over very little. The problems are overwhelming and exacerbated by racism. The solutions for the current urban problems are not intuitive. In an era when too much is expected from mayors, too little is available to them. Research cited in *Coleman Young and Detroit Politics* shows that mayoral initiative accounted for most of the city's current redevelopment projects. Yet from the outside, it appears as if the mayor merely implemented decisions made by others. In city politics, the increase in the number of black mayors is just part of the demographic history of America, not a sign of serious redistribution of the nation's economic resources. The same can be said about the mayor relationship with the school cartel.

NOTES

1. See Russell Murphy, "The Mayoralty and the Democratic Creed," *Urban Affairs Quarterly* 22 No.1 (September 1986): 3-23.

2. Interview with Coleman Young, September 8, 1994.

3. Robert Dahl, *Who Governs?* (New Haven: Yale University Press, 1961), p. 151.

4. Leigh Stelzer, "School Board Receptivity: A Representation Study," *Education and Urban Society*, 5 (November 1972), p. 80.

5. Interview with Richard Hatcher, op. cit.

6. Ibid.

7. Interview with Coleman Young, op. cit.

8. Interview with John Elliott, 1989.

9. Robert Salisbury, "School and Politics in the Big City, "*Harvard Educational Review* (Summer 1967), pp. 408-24.

10. See Paul Peterson, *The Politics of School Reform* (Chicago: University of Chicago Press, 1985).

11. See David K. Dunaway, "Desegregation and City Hall: The Mayor's Role in Schools," *Integrated Education* No. 85 (January-February, 1977):3-9.

12. Interview with Arthur Jefferson, April 17, 1990.

13. Bruce Alpert and Ron Russell, "Young Seeks School Changes," *The Detroit News* (September 10 1987), p. 9.

14. Ibid.

15. "Who Should Run Our Schools?," *The Detroit News* (September 13 1987), p. 18.

16. Ibid.

17. Jerome Zeigler, "Should the Mayor Run the Schools," *City* 6 (Winter 1972), p. 17.

18. Ibid., p. 16.

19. James Scott, op. cit., p. 245.

20. Ibid., p. 247.

21. Interview with Arthur Jefferson, April 17, 1990.

22. Marion Orr, "Urban Regimes and School Compacts: The Development of the Detroit Compact," *The Urban Review* 25 No. 2 (1993), p. 119.

23. Ibid.

24. See Kenneth Kenitson, *The Uncommitted* (New York: Harcourt, Brace & World).

25. Willa Johnson, "Illusion of Power: Gibson's Impact Upon Employment Conditions in Newark, 1970-1974," (Unpublished Doctoral Dissertation, Rutgers University), p. 185.

26. N. John More, "From Dreamers to Doers," *National Journal* 32 1, p. 372.

27. Ibid., p. 373.

28. See Clarence Stone, *Regime Politics* (Lawrence: University of Kansas, 1989).

29. Clarence Stone, "Preemptive Power: Floyd Hunter's Community Power Structure Reconsidered," *American Journal of Political Science* 32, No. 1 (February 1988), p. 83.

30. Ibid., p. 99.

31. See Georgia Persons, "Reflections on Mayoral Leadership," *Phylon* 46 (September 1985): 205-218.

32. See Jeffrey Pressman, "Preconditions of Mayoral Leadership," *American Political Science Review* 65 (June 1979): 11-24.

33. Craig T. Ladwig "When Newspaper Loses Identity," *The Detroit News* (November 19 1989) p. 15A.

34. See *Elrod v. Burns*, 427 U.S. 347.

35. Interview with Alonzo Bates, op. cit.

36. Wilbur Rich, "Coleman and Detroit Politics, 1973-1986," in *The New Black Politics,* Michael Preston, Lenneal Henderson, and Paul Puryear (New York: Longman, 1987).

37. Jerry Hagstrom, " Mayoral Candidates Enter the Big Times: Costly TV Ads and Consultants," *National Journal* 17 (1985), p. 737.

38. See John Mollenkopf, *The Contested City* (Princeton, N.J.: Princeton University Press, 1983).

39. See Dennis Judd and Todd Swanstrom, *City Politics* (New York: Harper Collins, 1994).

40. See Terry Adams, Greg Duncan, and Willard L. Roger, *Quiet Riots: Race and Poverty in the United* States (New York: Pantheon, 1988).

41. Wilbur Rich, *Coleman Young and Detroit Politics: From Reform to Power Brokers* (Detroit: Wayne State University, 1989), p. 92.

CHAPTER 6

Rust-Belt Cities and Their Green-Belt States

In the late sixties black politicians asserted that their time had come. In the seventies, they began by electing a majority on local school boards. The dream came true in the late seventies, but the eighties were a nightmare. Their impassioned enthusiasm of the previous decade was replaced by angst. The old anxiety was that whites would continue to make it difficult for blacks to make school policy through financing and state law. The new anxiety was that black school administrators and leaders would fail to demonstrate any improvement in student performance, creating a demand for yet another takeover. The most foreboding fear was that schools under black control might contribute to the economic paralysis of the black underclass.

This chapter analyzes the complex relationship between state governments and school districts. I will examine the states of Indiana, Michigan, and New Jersey vis-à-vis Gary, Detroit, and Newark, respectively. The central issue is why states do not play a greater role in local district affairs in light of the continuing failure of inner city schools. In the past states have played mainly fiscal roles, with very little oversight of local units. Where does local incompetence stop? A review of state-local relationship will explain the organic nature of this process and whether new thinking and relationships are apparent.

In one of the first textbooks on city government, Austin F. MacDonald (1941) posed the question: What degree of control should state authorities exercise over local school system?

> Education is more than a purely local problem. The
> state is vitally interested in guaranteeing to every one

155

of its inhabitants the opportunity to secure an adequate
preparation for his life work. It cannot afford to give
each community free rein, for the result would be local
anarchy. Some school systems would be brought to a
high pitch of efficiency, while others would speedily
degenerate. On the other hand, the people of every city
are vitally interested in their local educational
problems. The school system is a matter of local
concern, and a source of local pride. It would be a
serious mistake to vest all control over school affairs
in state officials. The best plan, apparently, is to permit
each community to establish and maintain its own
school system, but to retain in state hands the right to
fix and enforce minimum standards.[1]

Richard Elmore, on the other hand, believes states are the most
significant part of the political economy: "States, a system of
resources, rules and institutions, are 'nested' in a larger set of
political and fiscal relationships with the federal government and
localities. These relationships are sometimes collaborative, and
sometimes dependent, but in the long run they maximize
constituent support, subject to constraints on resources."[2]

The Origins of a Complex Relationship

As Marshall et al.[3] have pointed out, the political culture of a
state determines the environment for the development of
educational resources. The history of Indiana, Michigan, and New
Jersey public schools suggests that they are progressive when
compared to other states. Daniel Elazar's typology has classified
political cultures of states in terms of moralism, individualism,
and traditionalism.[4] A moralistic political culture views politics
as competitive and healthy and that public interest is best served
by full participation of the entire public. Under this definition
Michigan could be classified as moralistic.

Michigan has never envisioned taking over the fiscal
management of the Detroit school system. Even in a conservative
state, there are attempts to provide the city with more resources
to achieve equity. An individualistic political culture views politics
as dirty. It focuses on accountability and governance. Hence the

threat of takeover of local school districts by state officials is a serious matter.

New Jersey is an industrialized state that has benefited from its proximity to New York City. The political culture has generated a very tough and conflictual type of school politics. Accordingly, New Jersey could be classified as an individualistic state. The tax revenue from the shipping and petro-chemical industries allowed the state to create and maintain a fairly successful and adequately funded K-12 system, but as the economy began to falter, it could not maintain its balance of school finance across the state.

Newark, once a major port city, has undergone a lingering economic downturn. The current plight of Newark schools belies the interesting history of public schools in the state. In 1676, Newark, the oldest of the three cities, established its first school in the city. It had a school system for two hundred years before the state established a statewide office. In 1866 New Jersey established its state board and named its first school officer. If the Dillon Rule (i.e., where the state has absolute power over its administrative creations) applies to municipalities, then it also applies to school districts. The Dillon Rule for districts was upheld in a New Jersey case, *City of Trenton v. New Jersey* (1923).[5] Since then, the state has taken over local school districts in times of fiscal mismanagement.

Michigan, although it began as a rural state, developed because of the industrial and manufacturing economies created by the automobile-related industries. The automobile industry continues to dominate the state economy. However, during the period of agrarian economy, the state led the nation in school reform. In 1835 Michigan became the first state to make the state superintendent a constitutional officer. In 1874, the state court, in the famous Kalamazoo Case, ruled that the state could use state funds to establish a public secondary school.[6] In 1905 the power of Michigan to consolidate districts was challenged in *Attorney General of State of Michigan Ex. Rel. Kies v. Lowrey.*[7] The U.S. Supreme Court declared that school districts, although they are public corporations, they are created by an act of the legislature "and they are sometimes unwillingly born."[8] If in the wisdom of the state legislature, consolidation is indicated, then local districts have no legal grounds to object.

In *Kuhn v. Thompson* (1921) the Michigan Court reasserted this principle.[9] In 1928 the Michigan Court held that any power a city exercises over a school district must be conferred by statutes. In 1931 the Court restated the idea that local units were mere instruments of state governments. In a study in the early sixties, Masters et al. concluded there was a lack of consensus about schools in the state.

> First, the education groups that make demands on the legislature are no longer unified. Second, the failure to adopt a state-wide school district reorganization plan immediately after World War II has resulted in a situation where the wealthy and poorer districts display a considerable self-consciousness over their conflicting interests, and these divisions are reflected and articulated with the legislature when school district reorganization or state aid is the issue. Third, there is a long-standing cleavage between two ideologically oriented parties. . . . Finally, it should be mentioned that there is a division between the proponents of public schools and the protectors of the parochial and private schools. This division seems to be based more on economic than religious grounds, but in any event it is largely latent at present.[10]

Their study compared Michigan with Illinois and Missouri of the 1960s. Although their comments remain relevant for the 1990s, the divisions now turn more sharply on an urban/suburban axis. There are still considerable disparities among districts. Detroit is not the only city in the state, but most of the legislative focus on schools revolves around what to do about this district.

Indiana, considered the most conservative state of the three states, has maintained its traditionalistic political culture. In 1890 the Indiana court was one of the first to define the power of the school boards. In *State ex rel. Clark v. Haworth,*[11] the state court held that a school board derives all authority from the state. Accordingly, such boards are restricted by state law and can only exercise those powers granted to them. The state retains the right to create, reorganize, and eliminate any school districts.

Schools as Special Districts

School districts are expected to govern themselves regardless of each district's relationship to its city charter. School boards, whether elected or appointed, have the legal authority to conduct school affairs. The quasi-corporation status of boards grants them the right to create contracts and hire staff without the approval of the states or city government. Although ultimately responsible to the authority of the state, school districts by tradition have autonomy. These powers cannot be abrogated to elected municipal officials. Although the supremacy of state legislatures over all aspects of local school policy has been confirmed by the courts, states have been very reluctant to restrict or second-guess decisions made by local school districts. When state legislatures enter the thicket of local school politics, they do so at their own peril. Even small changes in the legislation regarding local school districts may be regarded as an invasion of local autonomy. Local communities have readily accepted state financial aid but resent state oversight and mandates. Local district officials fear state interference more than do municipal officials. The public generally expects appointed school administrators to stay out of municipal politics. Conversely, they also expect mayors to stay out of school matters even in cases where the board is appointed by the mayor.

This separation of school and municipal politics is the espoused norm, although not the norm in practice. Increasingly, the fiction of separation has been faced with the reality of taxpayer revolts, school safety issues, and continuing race relations problems. Municipalities and school districts have often been at odds over fiscal issues, construction, the location of school facilities, and compliance with city laws. Disputes between schools and city halls are usually settled by negotiation or by the courts.

In theory, a determined and hostile mayor could turn public opinion against the leadership of the schools. Rarely has this happened because the leadership of the school system has generally been amenable to mayoral advice. In general, black mayors have been reluctant to take on the core of the local black middle-class, teachers. This relationship is not a mutual admiration society but rather one that maintains territorial integrity. In most cases the political elite and school cartel have muted criticisms of each other. Yet they need each other. School leaders see themselves as a part of a positive governing alliance. Any negative criticism has the potential of destroying the fragile relationship within the coalition. This reluctance was clearly demonstrated by the reactions of black mayors to the various crises in school policy.

What about state governments taking over control of a system once it has demonstrated it is not capable of self-management? Should the children of the poor have to bear the additional burden of having incompetent administrators and teachers? Can the state legislatures open up the reform process? Why can't the state solve the fiscal problems of the school? Is it possible to have full state funding with local control? These are questions people ask while searching for new solutions to the inner city school crisis. Unfortunately, solutions to the school crisis are counterintuitive, i.e., the obvious solutions seldom work. In other words, answers are not simple, nor can they be inferred from the documentation of mistakes. However, two generalizations can be safely made: local inner city districts cannot solve the fiscal crisis of their systems, and the current political environment works against any rational reform of current inner city systems. State governments have all the constitutional authority needed to reform its schools but none of the political resources they would take to make fundamental changes in city schools.

State departments of education staffs continue to grow in size and complexity. As the state legislature passes more state laws, more state fiscal rescues occur, but the authority of state departments of education's authority in local school affairs is constrained by tradition, law, and state politics. State superintendents do have more oversight but less political impact on local boards. Over the years the state has accumulated incredible amounts of data and statistics regarding the education process of local districts and its students, but it doesn't seem to be able to use this information to help its weak districts. Ironically, strong districts, i.e., those which are financially strong, benefit the most from any additional services rendered by the state. Weak districts are the most politicized and hence the most insulated from effective oversight from state departments. District leaders not only inherited a tradition of autonomy from their predecessors but have also sought and secured more independence from the state capitols—Lansing, Trenton, and Indianapolis.

State-local district relationships are getting more complex each year. The organizational paralysis of inner city schools has its origins in the evolution of public education in America. What was once a simple matter of teaching children how to read, write, and figure is now a complex set of institutional arrangements supported and defended by self-serving interest groups. These interest groups, particularly teacher unions, have not only gotten their way politically, but their victories have been institutionalized into law. By defining all relations with the board as labor issues and bargainable, they get the extra coverage benefits of the state labor laws. The state also has passed laws about school bonds, laws preempting the board for passing residence requirements, and bidding procedurals for public contracts. These new laws are added to a series of court decisions which make for a very complicated intergovernmental relationship. This situation prompted A.P. Johnson and Raymond Proulx to conclude that the "present rationalized legal and political grounds for effective operation of the organization cannot alone carry the weight of knowledge which is required for effective operation of the organization."[12] Rather, what is required is the conceptual "complexization of the tasks to be done in education as a first step in sorting out the role that state policy can play most effectively."[13]

Governors and Mayors

It is useful to discuss the development of the governor as an exponent for education within the state. Following the lead of Lamar Alexander of Tennessee, Thomas Kean of New Jersey, and Terry Sanford of North Carolina, governors have continued to take positions on school issues. The former Republican governor of Michigan, William Milliken, wanted to appeal the local busing ruling in Detroit, causing state Senator Coleman Young to denounce him as "modern day equivalent of George Wallace," the Alabama governor who blocked the school house to prevent integration.[14] The relationship between these two men changed as Young became Mayor and Milliken became a reliable supporter of financial resources for Detroit.[15] They became known as the "odd couple." However, mayors in general were beginning to share the education reform spotlight with governors.

Are these governors filling a vacuum that is left by the mayors? The answer to this question is that the office of governor has grown since the end of World War II. Governors now enjoy national visibility and, more importantly, statewide visibility. The statewide television networks put them in touch with the entire state in minutes. As the population shifts to the suburbs, the governors have become the spokespersons for the middle class. Many types of school issues are now decided at the state level because former President Reagan supported the notion that educational initiatives should be from the state level. Yet in a public opinion poll, Marshall et al. (1989) found that governors in their six state survey (Indiana, Michigan, and New Jersey not included) that governors rank below teacher organizations and just above legislative staff in their influence in school policy.[16]

The mayors of our cities have a lot of visibility in school politics. They lack the size of the governor's bully pulpit, and they have little appeal outside their cities. Even in New Jersey, where the governor competes with New York State politicians in the New York media, his or her news-making opportunities are better than the mayor of the state's largest border city. This is also true in Gary. In Detroit the mayor dominates local media coverage, but as the next chapter suggests this did not help him much with the school cartel.

The state was a larger tax base and therefore seems to be the logical place to locate funds for schools. As a result, mayors have been supplicants in the search for funds. Mayors Kenneth Gibson, Richard Hatcher, and Coleman Young were perceived as always asking for more money, whereas the governors are seen as trying to establish some fiscal responsibility in the cities. One might use the metaphor of governor as the fireman and the mayor as the man who ignored the arsonists. When former President Bush convened the nation's governors, the meeting seemed to highlight governors as the problem solvers in education. Accordingly, the continuous rivalry between the highest elected office in the largest city and the highest elected official of the state now includes school policy. Subsequently, the mayors are often ignored in negotiation among the education interest groups.

State Legislatures and Schools

State legislatures also exercise plenary power over curriculum and complete control over school property and personnel certification. Before the 1960s these powers were rarely challenged. The rural-dominated legislature perpetuated many outdated notions of school policy. Many resisted the state's taking the lead in integrating the schools. Since *Baker v. Carr* (1962),[17] there has been a revolution in the composition of state legislatures.[18] They are now considerably more cosmopolitan and less rural. In New Jersey there was a decided shift of power to suburban legislators.[19] In each of the three states partisan politics has been an influence in school policy making. The rise of black political power has changed the equation of school politics at the state level. Now Detroit, Gary, and Newark are considered '"the black problems." Legislative speeches are full of references to low student achievement, high school dropouts, and teenage pregnancies. More school money is viewed as "throwing money at social problems."

The problem is made more complicated if the city has a majority black population. Suburban state legislators consider black residents as a Democratic constituency. Republican state legislators often feel obligated to defend the suburban advantages in school funding and to support conservative solutions to school problems.

The education lobby is also considered Democratic as is organized labor. The teacher associations and unions receive support from both groups These groups have large constituencies and play a high profile role in state campaigns. The real power of school policy is located in the education committees of the state legislature. As the issue of school policy becomes more complex and costly, more highly-trained staff members are recruited to assist in the formulation of school policy. In some cases, outside consultants are engaged to study and report on issues before the legislature. Hence the staff members of these committees are courted by the education lobby. This is not to say that old-fashioned pork barrel politics are a thing of the past but rather that lawmaking has become more complicated. Individual legislators, considered full-time legislators in Michigan and New Jersey, can still make a difference in school policy. Masters et al. concluded that state legislators had little to gain from school politics and that most legislators ignored education politics as they prepared for higher office.[20] This is not the case today, as school politics is an easy and low-risk way of gaining visibility. The fact that education interest groups are reliable sources of campaign finance has not escaped the attention of candidates.

The advantages that Detroit, Newark, and Gary enjoy in school policy revolves around a bloc of urban legislators. In 1964 Masters et al. pointed out that when this bloc of urban legislators is unified, it "is able to bargain and negotiate with outstate legislators for the special legislation Detroit needs and desires."[21] The unity is still there, but cities have suffered massive population losses and hence enjoy less clout. Despite the urbanization of some of the city's inner suburbs, there is no organized interdistrict coalition to support schools in the metropolitan Detroit area, which consists of McComb/Oakland/Wayne Counties. There is also no such coalition with Gary and Newark metropolitan area. These cities have had to make their appeals on ground of moral equity. This appeal has become more complicated by the rising cost of schools and dwindling school populations.

Public schools are the largest single item in the state budget. State legislatures finance school districts primarily through local taxes on real estate property. School funds are legally state funds. The state can also impose limits on indebtedness. Michigan imposes a limit on gross debt but no limit on taxes to repay loans. Its laws state that if the school district exceeds 7 mills, the state is responsible for the excess. The conventional wisdom is that when the cost of indebtedness exceeds 15% of current operating expenditures, the local tax structure cannot raise enough revenue to support the system. The inability of local taxes to support the schools usually leads to deterioration in quality.

The financial problems of schools are by-products of unreliable income sources (property taxes), escalating union contracts with cost of living allowances, and poor fiscal planning. As the tax bases erode and taxpayers balk at higher tax rates, schools have been forced to make unpleasant fiscal adjustments. The fiscal problems have been exacerbated by the growing tendencies of taxpayers to take out their anger at higher taxes in general by voting against school millages as a whole. Voters are more angry at deficits than they are at teachers and their unions. Many are opposed to redistribution and equalization schemes to provide more money to poor districts. Aside from wanting to reduce their tax burden, there is no way to show the money will end the rampant inefficiencies in the schools. Eric Hanushek makes a telling point regarding this issue.

> One might argue that altering existing financing formulae would have only distributional consequences, because expenditure variations do not relate to the performance of different school systems. But this is not the only effect. The politics of redistribution tend to promote increases in total spending on schools. States find it difficult to lower funding for one district in order to raise it for another, and therefore they tend to raise low spending districts up to the level of high spending districts. (This probably explains the general support by teacher unions for school finance "reform.") The responses of states to challenges to their funding of schools are thus frequently to increase the amount of economic inefficiency in the system.[22]

Accordingly, increasing the amount of money available will not improve efficiency of schools, but it will alter the political calculations of the interest groups in the city. Public schools by nature are inefficient organizations. They don't maximize student achievement so much as they legitimate advantages students bring with them to class.[23] Therefore, there is significant amount of symbolic politics in the state equalization controversy. When city politicians talk about funding equalization, they are making a pitch for distribution policy. When suburban legislators fight to keep the extant formulas, they are making a pitch to property tax sensibilities of their constituency. Increased expenditures by themselves will not close the learning gaps between the two school systems.

Legislatures as Mediators of City/Suburban Conflict

There are 303 school districts in Indiana, 563 in Michigan, and 604 in New Jersey. Once the decision is made to create a district, it is very difficult to terminate the unit. Each district has its own school board unless there is an authorized merger of districts. Students are restricted to their attendance zones in their district of residence unless otherwise authorized. In Detroit parents have been prosecuted for faking their residency in order to enroll their child in a suburban school. Keeping the inner city students contained has become a major preoccupation of state legislators.

The battle over interdistrict busing was won with *Milliken v. Bradley* (1974).[24] The court ruled that the Detroit Metro Busing Plan was not required by the U.S. Constitution. This ruling has turned district lines into blockades. If this case had gone the other way, state governments would have been forced to act as coordinators of busing plans. Maintaining the integrity of the existing districts is a much easier task. These barriers also helped suburban communities to market schools as drawing cards for new residents. Paul Peterson, in *City Limits*, suggests that the social equity norms of inner-city schools put them at a disadvantage when competing in the metropolitan marketplace for new residents.[25]

Today the primary struggle between central cities and suburbs is over the state formula. There seems to be a consensus that inner cities need more state aid and that a state's largest city should be treated as a special case. However, this conflict has sharpened as the state has attempted to meet the fiscal problems of city schools. Aside from a weak tax base, the selected cities in this study have also been accused of mismanagement of funds.

Suburban communities fight most equalization formulas. Empowered by the *Baker v. Carr* (1962)[26] ruling that required a one-man, one-vote reapportionment of state legislatures, these communities have created a working coalition with rural districts to keep the status quo. Despite incessant fiscal crises of inner city schools, there has been resistance to alternative funding mechanisms. In 1968 Arthur Wise's book *Rich Schools—Poor Schools*[27] promoted the notion that the right to equal education could not be protected under the unequal funding process. Equity in school finance is impossible if the property tax is the base for school funding. In 1972 the New Jersey State Court, with *Robinson v. Cahill*,[28] followed the famous *Serrano v. Priest*,[29] which declared state laws which based school funding on property taxes unconstitutional. In *Serrano* the case was made that property tax financing violated the equal protection of the Fourteenth Amendment because it was biased toward wealthy districts. Education is a fundamental interest of all citizens of California. However, the U.S. Supreme Court, in a plurality decision, reversed *Serrano* in *San Antonio Independent Schools et al. v. Rodriquez et al.* (1973).[30] In effect the Court said that education was not a "fundamental interest." The wealth of the state, not the district, should determine the financing of public education. However most states continue to use property taxes as the primary funding source for schools, and the disparities among districts continue to increase.

What if there was full state funding? Would that eliminate the blatant disparities in equipment, cost-per-student, and teacher salaries? Could inefficient districts be eliminated? Would full state funding retard the level of funding for wealthy districts? Wealthy districts have used this argument to resist the equalization movement. However, wealthy districts could offset any changes with supplemental provisions for teachers. The real fear is the loss of local control. Accordingly, the state legislature has stayed out of the financial thicket in order to avoid political reactions. A go-slow policy may be wise because of the rising cost of schools. In addition, there is no consensus about what school districts like Detroit, Gary, and Newark would need to make them competitive with their suburban counterparts. State legislators believe that the best strategy is to do nothing until the question of school financing is finally settled by the courts.

Growth of State Regulatory Power

The purpose of regulation is to maintain standards, protect local districts from local politics, protect teacher and student rights, and promote social justice. The literature on state departments of education concentrates on education leadership, service to local units, and the role of education in the state economy. The role of the state superintendent is a by-product of a state's political history. John G. Richardson believes that the history reveals the capacity of a state system for change and development. He believes that compulsory school attendance laws mark the beginning of state oversight of local systems.[31] Michigan's compulsory school law was first passed in 1871, New Jersey's in 1875, and Indiana's in 1897. Until the turn of the century the role of state departments was limited to inspecting local schools. New functions were added as the federal government started funding vocational education with the Smith-Hughes Act of 1917.

Before World War I, state education superintendents and boards of education maintained a low profile in local school politics and finance. In 1908 Michigan established its state board of education. Elected at-large on a partisan statewide ballot, the current board members serve a staggered term with two members elected every two years. The elected members are voting members. The governor and the state superintendent are ex-officio members of the board. In our three states, the law requires that the state department provide the legislature with an annual report and the data on local districts. The state offices monitor various legislative proposals proffered by interest groups. The power of the state to regulate local boards was confirmed in *Oliver v. Kalamazoo Board of Education* (1972).[32]

Two important sources of state control include the areas of teacher certification and school curriculum. The state retains the power to certify teachers and to determine tenure and promotions. This power was reaffirmed in *Welling v. Board of Education for the Lovania School District* (1969).[33] The state legislature can require that civic education be taught in every school. The state legislature is continually faced with demands for more content in the curriculum. Michael Kirst believes that this has led to the current curricular "smorgasbord," which requires the schools to provide too many services.[34]

During the sixties blacks began to press for the inclusion of their racial histories in approved American history textbooks. This move has been met with enormous resistance. Although blacks in the three selected cities control local boards, they cannot arbitrarily revise the curriculum or teacher qualifications.

The New Jersey state board of education is appointed by the governor with the advice and consent of the state senate. Members serve without compensation for six-year terms. There are thirteen voting members, including representatives from the board of higher education and the chancellor of higher education. State law requires that three members be women. Each member must be from a different county. The state commissioner of education acts as the secretary of the board and its chief administrative officer. The state board promulgates rules for implementation of state school law, hears appeals concerning school disputes, and oversees local districts.

In the cases of the *Board of Education of Elizabeth v. City Council of Elizabeth* (1970)[35] and *Board of Education of East Brunswick Township v. Township Council of East Brunswick* (1966),[36] the courts decided that state officials can overrule local municipal officials (e.g., city councils) if their school budgets do not meet constitutional requirements. Michael Santaniello believes these two court rulings are a clear threat to local control of schools. The ruling gave the municipal governing body and the state department the authority to overrule the electorate. The courts empowered the state board to apply administrative review standards on appeals. Santaniello believes these rulings were the inevitable end of local control. He points out that voters can vote to reduce the school budget only to have it overruled by the state department of education. Santaniello asks, "By what authority can voters be overruled by an appointed body if in a democratic system all authority emanates from the people?"[37] His concern is that their board members were not required to be lawyers and hear appeals and that judgments may be unduly influenced by the state commissioner. The cases have "advanced the movement of centralization of power in the position of the Commissioner."[38]

If state mandates subordinate local districts, what about the amenability of local districts to state control? Have state agencies been captured by local district school policy makers? Is this a case of the local controlling the state department? The answers to these questions are not so simple as they seem. Aside from a tradition of local control, state government is only beginning to regain respect. Ann O'M. Bowman and Richard C. Kearney's book *The Resurgence of the States* suggests that new state initiatives are the result of state constitutional reform, more intergovernmental lobbyists such as the National Governors Association, reapportionment decisions, the decline of the state's largest cities as rivals of political power, and the withdrawal of the federal government from some domestic issues.[39] Larry Sabato's research suggests that states are recruiting more competent governors who see themselves as national figures and managers.[40] The Educational Governance Project, which included the state of Michigan, found that the government used education financing not only as a way to provide tax relief but also as a way to achieve more control over policymaking in education. State legislatures have also improved. Since public education is one of the largest items in the state budget, it has received more attention from governors and state legislators.

The teacher unions have emerged as the primary defenders of local autonomy and increased state aid. By allowing union lobbyists unfettered access to policy making, the state department has been reduced to a fiscal policy crisis manager and chief lobbyist for more state aid. State superintendents who act as problem-solvers are often criticized by all parties in school disputes. Yet these superintendents worked to allow more state aid to local districts. This state aid remains the largest and most costly distributive policy. The recent taxpayer revolt has seriously undermined the state department/local district coalition, which lobbies support for school funding. Efforts to promote more aid have been hindered by incessant stories of unethical behavior, mismanagement, and poor school performances. Unfortunately, states have not done much to alleviate this problem. Sroufe contends that the problem of oversight and "applying sanctions is always controversial and withholding of funds injures those most needing, assistance."[41]

The state education department's ability to conduct effective oversight over local districts is hampered by a small staff, rivalry with state legislative education committees, and uncertainty about the proper role of the state chief education officer. Without this role clarity, department legitimacy suffers. It doesn't seem to matter whether the state chief officer is appointed by the governor or by the state board of education. Elected superintendents do not seem to fare any better than their appointed counterparts. In one of the first books on state departments, Lee Thurston and William Roe concluded that "it is an error to suppose that an educational official will gain strength from periodic contact with the people at election time. Getting elected is so pleasing an experience as to sharpen the average appetite for more political conquests of the same sort and to cause an official to steer his course accordingly."[42]

The Role of the State Superintendent

Appointed by the state board of education, the state superintendent in Michigan acts as the governor's watchdog in local districts. In theory the superintendent works for the state board of education, but he is also a member of the governor's cabinet and administers the largest part of the state budget. He is the chairman of the state board and promulgates district reporting rules and regulations.

In 1984 Indiana created its first state board of education. The governor appoints the eleven-member board, which by law must consist of members representing each Congressional district. Only six of the ten can be of the same political party. Four of the members must be professional educators. The state board sets the educational goals of the state. It also supervises the distribution of state education funds, accreditation of local schools, teacher certification, and textbook adoption. The Indiana superintendent of public instruction is a voting member and chairman of the board. In addition to advising the governor and the state legislature, he or she also appoints advisory committees to the board.

In New Jersey, the education commissioner is appointed by the governor and serves in the cabinet. The commissioner is in charge of apportioning state aid to local school districts, conducts statewide tests, promulgates rules for handicapped children, and provides oversight over local districts. Because New Jersey does not have a history of strong city government or independent schools, the superintendents have more political power than do their counterparts in other states.

The state superintendency has become a major political position since blacks gained control over local boards. This is primarily because predominantly black districts are financially unstable and school politics in those cities are highly conflictual. Blacks lack political strength statewide, making them somewhat vulnerable to outside intervention. Increasingly, state departments have intervened in the affairs of weak districts to force the administration to adopt a balanced budget. In all three cases, the states have done numerous studies of district finances.

State law provides that in cases of a fiscal collapse, the state would become the receiver of the system. During the Detroit 1988 school fiscal crisis, the specter of state takeover was used as a threat to generate support for the local board. The system had run up an incredible deficit; board members were publicly fighting amongst themselves, and Detroit school kids had the worse reading and math scores in the state. Susan Watson, a black columnist for the *Detroit Free Press*, was one of the first journalists to break ranks by reporting that the superintendent's warning of state takeover was greeted by citizens as a welcome change.[43] The state was not anxious to take over the schools but sought more authority in district affairs. A state takeover, initiated for Newark and implemented in Jersey City, has done little to change the relative influence of interest groups, to say nothing about the quality of education. There is no evidence that state takeovers can rebuild school systems. Such actions are only a tourniquet for rapid-flowing red ink. They are no substitute for a weak tax base. Such dramatic actions serve to place the state in the spotlight. In a few cases these actions caused the governor to become more involved.

In general, governor's offices have become very active in school policy decisions. During Michigan Governor Blanchard's tenure, the state treasury department became a critical player in school finance. The treasurer's office has become more vocal about district affairs since it is in the position of certifying school bond offerings. The governor's role in public education has also been advanced by his own initiatives in public education. Former Governor Richard Riley of Tennessee, President Clinton's Education Secretary, remains a role model for some governors. President Bush had tapped the governors as point persons for his "proposals" for school reform. They, in turn, wanted the visibility of being seen as proponents of education reform. Former Governor Kean of New Jersey and G. Mennen William of Michigan were examples of governors with a strong interest in public schools, yet these prestigious leaders were unable to change the direction of school policy.

In all three states superintendents have been professional educators with little or no background in statewide politics. Many state superintendents are products of local school districts and perceive the job as the capstone of their career. A governor may want to use a superintendent as a promoter of his policies. Local school boards want a lobbyist for more state aid. The state departmental staff want more federal aid programs and a leader who will bring and retain prestige for the department. The legislature wants a budget analyst and in-house education expert. Increasingly state superintendents have been called upon to act as mediators for state legislative initiatives. This rings particularly true in the case of school finance and other redistribution policies. Increasingly state superintendents are asked to do more but are not given any more authority over local districts.

Impact of Federal Programs

Around the same time minorities began to enter cities in large numbers, the federal government began increasing the funding of local districts. In 1940 the Lanham Act provided funds for local districts if they could document war-incurred impacts on their tax base. After World War II, the Federal Assistance Laws (P.L. 874 and 817) were passed. These laws provided funds for school construction in areas where the childrens' parents worked or lived on federal properties. In 1958 Congress passed the National Defense Education Act, which increased science and math teaching in secondary schools. This act, passed during the Eisenhower Administration, was a direct reaction to the *Sputnik* success of the Russians. The new acts served to increase the size of the state departments of education. Dentler claims that the relationship between the state and local districts has always been characterized by ambiguity. He asserts that "prior to 1965, many state chiefs spent their best energies explaining the ambiguities in their historically and politically circumscribed scope of real authority."[44]

The big change came in 1965 with the Elementary and Secondary Education Act, followed by the 1967 Amendments to the Act. This was the first time Congress had ever appropriated over a billion dollars for education. The act, considered part of President Johnson's War on Poverty, was directed toward low-income children. Title II of the ESEA required the state to develop a plan of action. Title III allowed direct grants to local districts to encourage innovation. Title V of the ESEA was designed to strengthen state departments of education. It included planning and development and special project grants. Kenneth Smith surveyed all fifty states and concluded that Title V "has permitted substantial growth in the size of professional staff; it has contributed greatly to the operating budgets of the smaller departments . . . significantly to the operating budgets of larger department; and it has allowed the departments to undertake new programs, and it expanded programs previously deemed insufficient."[45] Title IV expanded the research activities allowed in schools and established new networks for the dissemination of research.

Donald Layton agrees with Smith's contention that the chief impact of federal laws has been an enlargement of the state departments of education.[46] State staff expansion has not increased the political clout or the professional credibility of these agencies. They are seen as check signers, not program designers. In effect, there has been a failure to regulate local districts, as the three case studies in this book demonstrate. John Chubb has argued that federal school grants between 1965 and 1979 have created a hierarchy of policy authority. He sees Washington as the principal innovator and the states as the agents and implementors of school policy.[47] This new alliance between the state and federal government crosses party lines.

Teacher Unions and State Politics

In all three cities, teachers are represented by the American Federation of Teachers (AFT). Local teacher organizations in Gary and Chicago came together in 1916 to form the AFT. However, the struggle for collective bargaining was difficult. Ironically, teacher unions got their initial success at the state level. Le Roy Ferguson found that teachers were effective as lobbyists before they were powerful forces in their respective cities. In 1957 New Jersey legislators relied on the education associations for information on policymaking and for advice about proposing new taxes for schools.[48] Teacher unions became a force in state government before they became active in municipal politics.

Today teacher unions have acquired considerable political clout in their respective state houses. They hold the ability to raise funds for supportive state legislators in every district. Part of the reason for their ascendancy in politics is the gaining of fund raising parity with private unions. The key case is *Abood v. Detroit Board of Education (1977)* in which the Supreme Court found that granting exclusive bargaining rights to a certified union by stature was constitutional.[49] Teachers unions now had an agency shop which meant all non-union teachers had to pay an agency fee to the union.

Although some rivalry exists between the National Education Association (NEA) and the American Federation of Teachers (AFT), particularly at the state level in Michigan, both have endorsed collective bargaining as a legitimate means of achieving teachers' goals. Collective bargaining allows teachers to obtain coverage under existing labor laws and to affiliate with national labor organizations.

State laws set the terms of labor recognition, elections, and exclusive representation. In some states, laws covering public schools prohibit the inclusion of administrators and teachers with the same bargaining units. The union has increased the state's role in education and local politics. Finn makes a similar argument.

> The teacher unions also enlarged the state's role by focusing on the capitols as the most promising places to gain added leverage for themselves—notably through collective bargaining laws and tenure laws, among others—and to press for salary increases and other direct benefits for their members. Widening union influence and mounting activism during the 1960s and 1970s thus tended to shift power from local school boards to the state house.[50]

In cities such as Detroit, teachers and principals have divided into separate bargaining units, creating a strange alliance. Although state laws prohibit strikes by teachers, the strikes in Detroit and Newark prove these laws are unenforceable. In the three cities in this study, the state labor laws differ in terms of the scope of bargaining, i.e., those items which are negotiable. In Michigan class size, salaries, benefits, and work rules are considered bargainable items. Indiana and New Jersey state laws impose some restrictions on these items. Despite differences in laws, teachers have amassed considerable political power in the three cities in the study. In many instances the teacher unions have used their political clout in a positive manner to push for more direct state aid, state equalization formulas, and an end to the reliance on the property tax as the core of school finance. At other times the teachers unions have lobbied to protect the complex relationship between the state and local districts which allowed them to maintain the interest of their allies in the school cartel.

Summary

Local control of schools has deep roots in the black community. There are three formal sources of power in school districts: state constitutions, state statutes, and case law. Accordingly, boards of education have no inherent powers. School districts are agencies of the state designated to perform a single state function. Schools become mere administrative devices for the exercise of state powers. Although boards are quasi-corporations, they were not designed as municipal corporations. Municipal corporations differ from school districts because they were created for purposes of self-government.

The courts repeatedly maintain the separateness of mayors and councils from school policymaking authority. The fact that a city charter empowers the mayor or the city council to appoint or confirm school board members does not make board members municipal officers. Legally school board members and their staffs are state officials. Politically, local school board members regard themselves as local officials. In Gary, where the board is appointed, members see themselves as mayoral appointees and extensions of the mayor's power. Before 1983 Mayor Gibson routinely had his appointees sign a resignation letter upon appointment. Therefore, all the mayor had to do was to date it and announce the resignation of the school board members. This letter was the mayor's attempt at insuring that his policy preferences were followed. These appointees, like most Newark residents, regard school board policy as a matter of local politics. Even when school politics mix with local politics, the board's status remains a state agency. The mayor, the appointing official in Gary, acts as a mere ex officio state official performing a state function rather than acting in a municipal capacity as mayor. Yet as we will demonstrate, politics reinforces the legal grounds for the independence of school boards.

School officials have little trouble rallying people around the notion that state houses are attempting to take away local control. Yet there is a growing consensus that state shares must increase appreciably to meet growing costs. State takeovers, once unspeakable, are now a part of the inner city political calculations of survival. The case studies of Detroit and Newark are examples of how this threat can be used to increase support for local control. Chris Pipho expressed the concern about increasing the role of the state education department in city school politics. He asserts "when cities add their weight to the political scales on behalf of a school district, unpredictable things sometimes happen. But when city and state officials move in concert to change a large-city school district, events become ever more unpredictable."[51] However, this type of state and local coalition is only episodically available for school reform. In these three case studies, unpredictability was the hallmark of Rust-Belt public schools.

NOTES

1. Austin MacDonald, *American City Government and Administration* (New York: Thomas Y. Crowell, 1941), pp. 510-511.

2. Richard F. Elmore, "The Political Economy of State Influence," *Education and Urban Society* 16 (February, 1984), p. 126.

3. Catherine Marshall, Douglas Mitchell and Frederick Wirt, *Culture and Educational Policy in American State* (New York: The Falmer Press).

4. Daniel Elazar, *American Federalism: A View from the States* (New York: Crowell, 1984), p. 120

5. *City of Trenton v. New Jersey*, 262 U.US 182(1923).

6. See *Stuart v. School District No. 1* of Kalamazoo, 30 Mich. 69 (1874).

7. *Attorney General of State of Michigan upon Relation of Kies v. Lowrey*, 199 US 233, 263, Ct. 27 (1909).

8. Ibid., p. 236.

9. *Kuhn v. Thompson* 134 N.W. 722 (Mich.1912).

10. N. Masters, Robert Salibury, and Thomas Eliot, *State Politics and Public Schools* (New York: Alfred A. Knopf, 1964), p. 180.

11. *State ex rel. Clark v. Haworth*, 122 Ind. 462 N.E. 946 (1890).

12. A. P. Johnson and Raymond Proulx, "State Education Policy: Old Rules, New Agenda," *Planning and Changing* 18 (Winter, 1987), p. 199.

13. Ibid.

14. Cited in Mirel, p. 349.

15. See Wilbur C. Rich, *Coleman Young and Detroit Politics* (Detroit: Wayne State University, 1989).

16. Marshall et al., op. cit. p. 22

17. *Baker v. Carr*, 369 U.S. 186 (1962).

18. See R. Dixon, *Democratic Representation* (New York: Oxford University Press, 1968).

19. T.G. O'Rourke, *The Impact of Reapportionment* (New Brunswick, NJ: Transaction Books, 1980).

20. Masters et al., op cit. p. 275.

21. Ibid., p. 199.

22. Eric Hanushek, "The Economics of Schooling," *Journal of Economic Literature*, 23 (September 1986), p. 1171.

23. See Pierre Bourdieu, *Outline of a Theory of Practice* (Cambridge: Cambridge University Press, 1977).

24. *Milliken v. Bradley* , 418 U.S. 717 (1974).

25. See Paul Peterson, *City Limits* (Chicago: University of Chicago Press, 1981).

26. *Baker v. Carr*, 369 U.S. 186 (1962)

27. Arthur Wise, *Rich Schools—Poor Schools: The Promise of Equal Educational Opportunity*, (Chicago: University of Chicago Press, 1968).

28. *Robinson v. Cahill*, 62 N.J. 473 (1973).

29. *Serrano v. Priest*, 96 Cal. Rptr. 601, 487 P 2nd, 1241, 5 Cal 3rd, 584 (1971).

30. *San Antonio Independent District et al. v. Rodriguez et al.*, 411 U.S. 1(1973).

31. John G. Richardson, "The American States and the Age of School System," *American Journal of Education* 92 (August, 1984): 473-503.

32. *Oliver v. Kalamazoo Board of Education* (D.C. 1972) 346 F. SUPP. 766.

33. *Welling v. Board of Education for Lovonia School Dist.* 171 NW. 2d 545,382 Michigan, 620 (1969).

34. Michael Kirst, *Who Controls Our Schools?* (New York: W.H. Freeman, 1984).

35. *Board of Education of Elizabeth v. City Council of Elizabeth*, 55 N.J. Reports, 501, 262 Atlantic Reporter 2, 881.

36. *Board of Education of East Brunswick Township v. Township Council of East Brunswick*, 48 N.J. 94, 223 Atlantic Reporters 2, 481.

37. Michael A. Santaniello, "The Subtle Move Toward Total State Control Of Schools and School Districts," *Seton Hall Law Review* 2 (1970), p. 189.

38. Ibid.

39. See Ann O'M. Bowman and Richard C. Kearney, *The Resurgence of the States* (Englewood Cliffs: Prentice Hall, 1989).

40. Larry Sabato, *Goodbye to Goodtime Charlie: The American Governor Transformed, 1950-1975* (Lexington: Lexington Books, 1978).

41. Gerald G. Sroufe, "Selected Characteristics of State Departments of Education," in *Strengthening State Departments of Education*, Roald F. Campbell, Gerald G. Sroufe, and Donald Layton, eds. (Chicago: Midwest Administration Center, The University of Chicago, 1967), p. 16.

42. Lee M. Thurson and William H. Roe, *State School Administration* (New York: Harper and Bro. Publishers, 1957), p. 115.

43. Susan Watson, "Jefferson's Threat May Net Answer," *Detroit Free Press*, (July 4, 1988), p. 3A.

44. R. A. Dentler, "Ambiguities in State and Local Relations," *Education and Urban Society* 16 (February 1984), p. 148.

45. Kenneth E. Smith, "The Impact of Title V on State Department of Education," in *Strengthening State Department of Education*, Roald F. Campbell, Gerald E. Sroufe and Donald Layton, eds. (Midwest Administration Center, The University of Chicago, 1967).

46. Donald H. Layton, "Historical Development and Current Status of State Department of Education," in Ronald F. Campbell, Gerald E. Sroufe and Donald Layton, eds. *Strengthening State Department of Education* (Chicago: Midwest Administration Center, 1967).

47. See John Chubb, "Federalism and the Bias for Centralization," *The New Direction in American Politics* , John Chubb and Paul Peterson, eds. (Washington, D.C.: Inst. Brookings, 1985).

48. Le Roy C. Ferguson, *How State Legislators View the Problem of School Needs: Cooperative Research Project No. 532* (East Lansing, Michigan, Department of Political Science, Michigan State University, 1960), p. 1.

49. *Abood v. Detroit Board of Education*, 431 U.US. 209 (1977).

50. Chester Finn, "Governing Education," *Educational Policy* 1 (1987), p. 306.

51. Chris Pipho, "Urban School Districts and State Politics," *Phi Delta Kappan* 69 (February 1985), p. 398.

CHAPTER 7

Schools, Human Capital, and Race

The era of American dominance of the international manufacturing market is gone. We are currently in a new era, the postindustrial society.[1] An inevitable consequence of this transition is economic dislocation, job elimination, and the winnowing out of weak economic production locations. Due to their high wage structures and changing demographics, Detroit, Gary, and Newark were among the first casualties of the national economic transition. Located in the centers of economic transformation, these Rust-Belt cities have not escaped the dreaded aftermath of economic decline—unemployment, crime, decline of the local tax base, racial polarization, and environmental decay. At first, city politicians thought the shrinking manufacturing base would be offset by a booming and growing service economy. This substitution has not happened. As a result many white workers left the inner city. Black residents were left holding the economic bag—and there are few jobs left inside. The federal government attempted to stem the tide with so-called urban development policies such as the Urban Development Area Grant, but these funds were ineffective. There was an accumulation of weak labor market participants in cities. The labor-intensive manufacturing jobs are gone forever.

The impact of the economic transition touched all aspects of city life, particularly the schools. Schools in these cities had provided workers with the requisite knowledge and socialization for work in the old economy. Their graduates became assembly-line workers in Detroit automobile plants, steel workers in Gary, and the dock workers in Newark. Migrants to Michigan and New Jersey came from all over the world in search of work. The growing industrialized economy created the wealth necessary to sustain

182

good public schools. With the end of this era, public schools in these cities were left with no guidance as to how to produce job-ready workers for a new and less labor-intensive economy. The steel mills, the garment industry, and the automobile plants had always been the workplace of choice for students with high school educations. Now corporations in home towns were hiring only a fraction of the available labor force. For black workers the loss of jobs brought more alienation from the workplace. White workers were faced with a choice of going to college or settling for menial labor jobs. Black high school graduates found it virtually impossible to find work, and white workers found it disheartening to settle for menial jobs.

The business community in these three cities, particularly in the 1970s and 1980s, was unsure where the local economy was going and who the economic winners would be. Their suppliers, including the schools, were asked to be patient. Political leaders were asked to be more entrepreneurial. The signals that the corporate sector gave schools were, in retrospect, mixed and misleading. Automobile corporation leaders could have stopped the loss of their market share, and it is doubtful whether they will ever recover their 1960s preeminence. The steel companies simply surrendered to foreign producers. The shift of manufacturing jobs to less-developed countries with cheap labor directly affects the ability of city dwellers to market themselves as workers. Events took control, and thousands of young blacks had to face the prospect of never being able to work in a factory.

There was a quiet panic in America's inner cities. Black middle-class families who had lived in Detroit and Newark for generations concluded they had to move, either to the suburbs or to another city. Whites accelerated their flight from the inner city and retail businesses followed. Some workers moved to the Southeast and Southwest. Schools were left with children of the unemployed, single-parent families, and welfare recipients.

What happened to these cities was gradual, and some would say, predictable. When the jobs left, so did the employable labor. This trend of moving where the jobs are has a long history in

America. Without an expanding job base cities like Detroit, Gary, and Newark could not attract residents.

Historical Context and Change

Every American city must have a job base for continued growth. The job base of Detroit was the automobile industry and its ancillary support industries. The city had a long history of being a staging area for automobile manufacturing. Located on the Great Lakes, Detroit could accommodate transportation of steel, glass, and rubber. Several smaller automobile manufacturers made cars in Detroit long before Henry Ford perfected the assembly line process and made cars affordable to the average working person. Eventually the small companies were bought out by General Motors, Ford Motor Corporation, American Motors and Chrysler.

Even before World War I, blacks were recruited from the farms to work in automobile factories for five dollars a day. Recruiters were sent to Mississippi, Georgia, and Alabama, and Detroit become the employment mecca for blacks. One could make a decent living in the city without a high school education. Although racism greeted blacks in Detroit, it was mild compared to what faced them in Alabama and Mississippi. Detroit offered more than a job, it was an escape from rural life and racial segregation. Henry Ford built company towns such as Inkster and Dearborn to house his workers. His company policy was very paternalistic and. afforded many blacks their first health and welfare services. Over a fifty-year span, the city grew from 250,000 to 1.8 million.

The decline of Detroit's automobile industry started in the early seventies, but it went unnoticed by the public until the oil embargo of 1974, which exposed the automobile companies' vulnerability to Japanese imports. The Big Four tried to reverse the situation by making better cars, but Americans were now comfortable with imports. Even workers in Detroit were buying imports. There was considerable dismay at the inability of the Big Four to mount a strategy against the imports. Meanwhile, the plants were phasing in robotics, dispersing assembly plants, and eliminating many assembly-line jobs. The new skills created by robotics required fewer and better-educated workers.

Gary—Good Location, No Resources

The smallest city in our study, Gary, lived at the mercy of the steel industry. The leaders of U.S. Steel selected the location for Gary because of its proximity to Chicago and Lake Michigan. The company laid out the town and donated most of the land for settlement. When this nation led the world in manufacturing, Gary was a "mighty mouse," but the city became to be called "Mickey Mouse" by some of its residents. Despite being at the center of industrial America, it never invested in itself to become a great city.

At its apex, the leaders of the steel workers union played an important role in city politics. Paul Tiffany cites the union settlement of 1959 as the turning point in the history of the American steel industry. He disagreed with other scholars that the cause of the demise of the industry was caused by mismanagement, planning errors, labor polices, and neglect of technology. He concluded:

> While not denying that managerial inefficiencies did exist, we nevertheless found serious shortcomings in the foresight of labor leadership as well as in various public policies that affected steelmakers in the postwar era. The federal government's continuing failure to appreciate the special circumstances surrounding manufacture of tonnage carbon steel, including the nature of international competition that face this sector, contributed significantly to the subsequent diminishment of industry performance. Moreover, the government's propensity to financially assist offshore producers despite the negative effects this might have on long-term domestic interest only worsened the situation.[2]

Newark: A Dubious Transition

Newark, the third city in our study, has been described by one resident as "America's incredible shrinking city, but its leaders' egos are growing."[3] The rhetoric of politicians belied economic trends in the city, as if talking could halt the process of decline. An inevitable correlate of job loss is loss of population.

The 1980 census showed a population decline of 16.4%—from 329, 248 to 275, 221. This represented a greater percentage loss than either Detroit or Gary. Political leaders believed that the population losses, particularly of blue collar workers, would be replaced by new migrants. They wanted the city to enter the service economy and go after the white gentrification crowd. Located just across the river from Manhattan, it was a natural location for young white professionals seeking low-cost housing. The optimism dissipated as events unfolded. Despite these competitive advantages, Newark could not shake its reputation as a corrupt city.

The election of Kenneth Gibson and the creation of the Gateway Project did not help the image of the city as crime-ridden and corrupt. Efforts at image remaking were not effective. This city, despite its Italian-American enclaves, was increasingly seen as being taken over by blacks and Puerto Ricans. The central business district was allowed to deteriorate, and the Gateway Project was able to maintain only a small portion of the retail market. One observer allowed, "What defined Newark was the Central Ward and that is where the cameras keep coming back."[4] The Central Ward contained most of the city's minority and poor population. The drama of these residents was much more compelling than that of the city's remaining white population.

Yet Newark remains an important port city. Port Newark and Port Elizabeth, administered by the Port Authority of New York and New Jersey, employed over 25,000 workers. Over 15 million tons of cargo a year go through the port. It was also the third largest insurance city. In 1977 Wilber Allen compared the city of Newark with its surrounding counties. According to his data, the city of Newark's share of the jobs in the area went from 14% in 1966 to 8% in 1976. He found also that the service sector was becoming a factor in the city's economy. He concluded:

> Approximately 7% of all the economic units, i.e., income generating units, are in the service-producing sector. The flight of industry from the city occurred during a period of substantial increases in wholesale and retail trade, small services and amusements, and

finance, insurance, and real estate. However, while these and other smaller industry groups experienced net expansion over this period, all of them reached an apex in their growth and then began to decline. Of the five groups in which this pattern is readily apparent (wholesale and retail trade, transportation, small services and amusements, finance, insurance, and real estate, and contract construction), the apex for four of them occurred during 1970, and for the fifth (wholesale and retail trade), during 1971. The decline in these industry groups can be generally attributed to the downward trend in the national economy in the early 1970s. It is the simultaneity of these phenomena which explains the facts that the number of economic units has increased in the city.[5]

Since Allen's analysis, cities like Newark were treated to the anti-city policies of Reagan and Bush. No cities can exist long without jobs for their residents. The welfare system has enabled some cities to maintain some citizens, but the forces of economic decline can be seen everywhere. All types of workers are leaving, and the cities are losing the type of families they can ill afford to lose. Public schools lose their most stable families.

Whites Leaving, Blacks Staying

The outward migration of white people preceded the declining economic base and the onset of black political mobilization. The election of black mayors was a reaction to these population losses as outward migration continued. The tiny bedroom communities that surround the central city began to grow and prosper. The quality of schools in these suburban communities improved with middle-class residents. Many middle-class whites simply wanted uncongested living space. After the riots of the late 1960s, personal safety also became a big issue for some whites. None of these explanations are mutually exclusive, but they help to analyze the multidimensional aspects of white middle-class flight. Working-class whites living on the borders of the inner city felt most threatened. They did not have the resources to keep non-white ethnics out of their communities. With the people moving out of the city proper and fear of crime in the city escalating, many retail merchants followed people to the suburbs. Office employment changed as professional service workers such as physicians and lawyers also moved to the suburbs.

The job shift left minorities with limited job search strategies, since most could not move to the suburbs with the jobs. Whites didn't want them as neighbors. American cities were speeding down the road of hyper-segregation. Demographers Douglas Massey and Nancy Denton concluded the three cities in this study were among most racially segregated in America. The five dimensions of hypersegregation include: unevenness (i.e., blacks are overrepresented in some areas and underrepresented in others), isolation (i.e., little or no residential contact with blacks), clustering (i.e., blacks living in contiguous enclaves), centralization (i.e., blacks concentrating in one area of the city), and concentratio⁻ (i.e., blacks locating near the central business district).[6] Given these dimensions, Detroit, Gary, and Newark ranked very high in each of these criteria.

In 1989 Detroit, Gary, and Newark metropolitan areas showed race segregation percentages of over 75% in nearly every category. Gary had a 56% clustering score. Newark had a 69% isolation score. These cities were clearly among the most hyper-segregated areas among thirty metropolitan areas.[7] In a later study the authors blamed this hypersegregation on unrelenting housing discrimination. The implications of these entrenched housing patterns are that black school children now live in a social environment isolated from white America. This social isolation imposes a heavy compensatory and social burden on inner city teachers.

Schools often fight losing battles as jobs continue to leave the city. Those blacks who try to follow the jobs to the suburbs discovered that either local banks would not approve them for mortgages (red-lining) or neighbors resented them for moving in. Most black inner-city workers are forced to commute to the suburbs. The transportation costs increasingly eat into take home pay. Long bus rides, leaving home early, and arriving home late became the norm, causing disruptions in family life. Studies suggest that access to suburban jobs via the transit system does not solve the unemployment problem.[8] The jobs offered in the suburbs were minimum wage or slightly above, and many blacks did not have an incentive to make these long trips as there was little hope of economic advancement. These workers have little investment in their human capital. Ironically, inner city schooling is almost useless in improving job search strategies in a rapidly changing economy.

Underdeveloped Human Capital

The concept of human capital is central to the economics of education and to understanding the relationship of the labor market to schools.[9] Human capital represents an investment by the individual in education and training for the purpose of maximizing future income. Finishing high school, college, or graduate/professional training represents assets that should determine future earning potential. The more educational assets one has, the greater the chances one will increase one's earning capacity over a lifetime. Supposedly, investment in education benefits both the individual and the employer. Educated workers are thought to be more productive than uneducated ones. However, there are widespread misconceptions in this standard line of reasoning. This is not to say the business community is unaware of the human capital problem. Many business publications have been sounding the alarm for years. For example, *Business Week* magazine asserted:

> America, in short, has been scrimping on human capital. After trying to solve its serious competitiveness problems by pouring hundreds of billions of dollars into capital equipment, the country is discovering that it has been blindsided when it comes to workers. Corporate restructuring and a sharply cheapened dollar may have arrested the economic decline, but investing in people is turning out to be only way to reverse it.[10]

It is commonly accepted that socio-economic status (SES) largely determines who succeeds in school and training programs.

The inequality of society is writ large in the educational arena. Individuals with low SES are least able to make educational investments in themselves. Pierre Boudieu, a sociologist, called this the advantage that the middle class enjoy in school cultural capital. He claims that middle-class children have a linguistic and cultural advantage that allows them to decode the learning materials used in schools.[11] These differences in speech patterns, attitudes, and appearance serve to alert teachers to class position. Once alerted, teachers often make expectations based upon distinctions along class lines. In other words, they expect less from poor children and they ultimately get less.

The lack of education represents a gatekeeping device which enables employers to identify and sort out the poor. An employer assumes that the completion of high school or college is evidence of internalization of so-called middle class white values. Stereotypes about minority workers last a long time in the workplace. Employers are also inclined to hire minority people who closely match existing white workers. Accordingly, the white employer then screens for the "right kind of minority person." Can he or she fit in with the other workers? Are they sufficiently work oriented? Do they share white values? These narrow hiring standards restrict the numbers of minority workers and encourage tokenism.

Public school teachers and administrators may understand these hiring dynamics, but they are powerless to eliminate tokenism and job discrimination in the job market. They are also not inclined to tell students that only a few of them will get jobs and that employers favor people who look like them. When these issues come up in the classroom, teachers avoid the issue by stressing the intrinsic value of education.

Employment Changes in Detroit, Gary, and Newark

The decline of manufacturing jobs affects every sector of city affairs. Detroit lost 20.5% of its population between 1970-1980.[12] Most of these losses were white residents. The 1990 census indicated that they were followed by middle-class black residents.

Between 1977 and 1987, the percentage of manufacturing in the total economy fell from 34% to 25%.[13] Nevertheless, General Motors employs over 37,000 employees in the area, followed by Chrysler Corporation with 9,000 and Ford with 7,500.[14] The manufacturing base of the area economy has historically been concentrated in automobile parts and equipment. This job base is extremely sensitive to consumer spending. Detroit factories are selling a product that only disposable income can buy. When the nation is in a recession, Detroit enters a depression.

Detroit's service economy continues to grow, however. Between 1977 and 1987, the percentage of service jobs increased from 18.6% to 24.7%.[15] The city of Detroit is especially endowed with health services. Detroit Receiving, Harper, and Ford Hospitals are among the largest and most sophisticated health facilities in the world. William Beaumount Hospital, located in nearby suburban Troy, is one of the largest medical suppliers in the country. The phone, gas, and light companies grew with suburbanization and have become the largest employers in the metropolitan area. Detroit Edison has over 13,000 employees, followed by Michigan Bell with 5,100.

The economic decline of Gary, Indiana, parallels the decline of the steel industry, its largest employer. Gary continues to record the worst economic performance of the top 100 metropolitan areas. Over 35,000 steel jobs have been lost in the Gary/Hammond area. The city of Gary has suffered the most from the loss of steel jobs. Between 1977 and 1987 manufacturing jobs fell from 40% of the total number to 24.7%.[16] U.S. Steel, one the largest employers, has now slipped to second place in terms of numbers of employees. Inland Steel Harbor Works is the largest employer with 15,000 workers, twice the number of U.S. Steel.

> The problem for the municipality of Gary—its residents, social institutions and the former employees of the steel plants, their dependents and those who worked in the "downstream" local economy—is that the new steel plant employs only a small portion of workers from the old plants.[17]

The service industry in Gary, because of population losses, has not grown so fast as Detroit and Newark. In Gary, government employment represents 12.6%, wholesale and retail trade 15.7%, and health services 9.8%.[18] The largest employer in the area is the Northern Indiana Public Service. In the city of Gary proper, the largest employer is the school system and the Gary National Bank. United States Steel, now called the USX Corporation, had a decline in the number of jobs, from 35,000 in 1970 to 7,500 in the 1990s. Gary, a city of 180,000 in 1960, shrunk to 116,000 by 1990. The city has not been able to capitalize on its location near Chicago.

Newark has always had a stable employment base in the chemical industry (3.2% of total employment).[19] However, that industry is becoming more dispersed, particularly the pharmaceutical and toiletry industries. Newark's economy is reacting to this situation. The chemical industry's employment fell 2.6% between 1985 and 1987.[20] The total number of employees of big pharmaceutical companies like Hoffmann LaRoche, Merck and Company, and Warner-Lambert Company is about 15,000 workers. Allied Signal, maker of plastics, employs another 3,000 workers.

The electrical machinery industry, another critical part of the Newark economy which hires assembly-type workers, has also fallen off. Japanese imports have captured most of the market in televisions, radios, and semi-conductors. Employment in this industry fell 6% annually.[21] Between 1977 and 1987, the manufacturing sector fell from 27% to 19% of the area's economy.[22]

Newark's political elite understood some of these changes and attempted to shift to a service economy. Changing economies in one generation is not an easy task. In 1987 services expanded from 19.4% of all jobs to 25.5%.[23] Newark is just one of the beneficiaries of the growth of white-collar jobs in the New York metropolitan area. There are competitor cities in Connecticut. Hence, the city's growth remained anemic. The metropolitan area had only 1.6% annually employment growth. After 1982, growth did not improve substantially. Between 1983 and 1987, Newark ranked 79th among the top 100 metropolitan areas.[24]

Like Detroit, Newark's economy is moving heavily into the service economy. Business and administrative services account for 20% of the area's jobs. Wholesales and retail trade make up another 20%. Newark's proximity to New York gives it a major advantage over other cities in the Northeast. The Prudential Insurance Company has been primarily identified with the city of Newark. It employs almost 40,000 workers. Between 1983 to 1987 finance and insurance companies accounted for 11,500 new jobs in the city.[25] The next largest employer is AT&T with 12,000 workers, followed by Public Services Enterprises with 8,776, Bell Laboratories with 6,800, and Foster Wheeler Construction with over 5,000 workers.[26] In addition, Newark International Airport employs thousands of workers and handles more flights than either JFK or LaGuardia.

The statistics look better than the actual job situation. The number of unemployed black males has reached pandemic proportions. Black males have found the service economy even more of a competitive labor market. Fewer prestigious service jobs will mean more white educated people are competing for fewer status jobs. Accordingly, those black males who want to stay in Detroit, Newark, and Gary run the risk of being unemployed for a longer period of time.

The Effects of Prolonged Unemployment

Depopulation and out-migration are among the negative consequences of job loss. Whites began moving in the early sixties and accelerated their activity with the onset of racial violence in 1967 and 1968. Blacks began taking over the municipal government in the early seventies. By the eighties the takeover was complete. Peter Eisinger characterized these takeovers as "transracial displacement."[27]

The political takeover did not arrest the declining economic conditions for blacks. At the peak of the ascendancy of black mayors in the 1970s, a major recession hit the nation. Poor people suffered most during the recession and job losses. The War on Poverty was lost for lack of federal dollars, commitment, and know-how. Cities like Detroit and Gary became war torn and never recovered. Jeremy Rifkin paints an even more threatening picture of advance machine surrogates taking the place of repetitive work entirely. Artificial intelligence and robotics are advancing at a rapid speed. Rifkin believes the pace has left workers unprepared for the transition.

> Most workers feel completely unprepared to cope with the enormity of the transition taking place. The rash of current technological breakthroughs and economic restructuring initiatives seem to have descended on us with little warning. Suddenly, all over the world, men and women are asking if there is a role for them in the new future unfolding across the global economy. Workers with years of education, skills and experience face the very prospect of being redundant by the new forces of automation and information. . . . They wonder if they will be next to be replaced by the new thinking machines.[28]

Following the lead of Sidney Wilhelm's 1977 classic *Who Needs the Negro?*, Rifkin believes the current "technological unemployment had fundamentally altered the sociology of America's black community."[29] To avoid the abyss of permanent joblessness and underclass membership with its concomitant social pathologies, black mayors and white allies have mounted economic development strategies.

Economic Development Strategies

Mayors Ken Gibson, Richard Hatcher, and Coleman Young tried to reverse the effects of job losses. They asked for federal help and solicited investors to build in their cities. With the 1980 election of Ronald Reagan, all hopes of getting larger amounts of federal aid vanished. Reagan shifted the nation's attention away from cities to military spending. The Reagan Administration terminated General Revenue Sharing and cut the rate of growth for many entitlement programs. Yet city economic development offices stayed open and scrounged around for more federal monies.

The biggest loss for cities in this study were the Urban Development Action Grants (UDAG).

Detroit used these grants to expand its convention center and build the People Mover (an elevated rail system) for the downtown area. More recently two large office buildings were built downtown. Detroit city officials supported a General Motor Plant within the city limits (in Poletown) and a Chrysler Jefferson Avenue Plant in the downtown area. Many parts of downtown have been rebuilt. Yet suburbs like Southfield and Troy continue to compete with the city for office buildings and retail stores.

Newark continues to benefit from its proximity to New York. The PATH train enables people to live in New Jersey and work in Manhattan. Newark still has strong downtown traffic, but it barely sustains retail businesses. The downtown Center Business District (CBD) collapsed from the competition of the suburban malls. Newark's CBD shows more signs of stability than Detroit or Gary, however. The Prudential Insurance Company, the city's largest corporation and key to its efforts of maintaining a downtown retail presence, began a downsizing of its corporate staff. In 1978 the headquarters staff went from 14,000 to 4,000. Abandoned stores and blight were quite visible in both cases. On paper Newark seemed to be perfect for rapid gentrification, but it has been eclipsed by Hoboken and other smaller towns. Newark does not have the resources for a full recovery.

Gary is geographically close to Chicago but has few significant economic connections. The decline in steel-related jobs robbed Gary of its reason for existence. The idea of Gary as the site for a third Chicago airport never materialized.[30] Having been blessed for years with well-paying union jobs, the city is now searching for new industries to stem the out-migration.

Economic Policies and Schools

The turmoil in the economy makes planning an economically rational curriculum difficult, if not impossible. In our society, schools are the only institution which reaches the entire population of potential workers. Public school teachers in our society have been maligned, and the economy has not been on their side. What are schools actually training people to do? Without an employment nexus, what is the incentive to invest more in human capital? What will be the returns on investment in cognitive skills?

In the last two decades, the negative reputation of inner city schools has paralleled the decline of the cities. The dropout rate is high at a time of disappearing low-skill jobs. Black males are now more likely to drop out and are more likely to get involved with the criminal justice system at an early age. Staying in school will not protect them from the arbitrariness of the labor market. Yet schools in these three cities continue to be baffled about how to make inner-city students perform better. As we saw in our case studies, there were endless newspaper stories about low reading and math scores. Every month brings a media story about school-related violence and exposés on the school board and administration.

Meanwhile, employers and companies have tried to disassociate themselves from the central city schools. Some considered the names of some schools—Newark's Central High School, Detroit's Mumford High School—a stigma because of their reputation for providing poor-quality education. Aside from a stigma, a systemic buildup of crime statistics reinforced the perception that schools are chaotic. The placing of security guards in schools is a reaction to the increased use of weapons, drug dealing, and gang violence. Every violent incident seems to make it more difficult to improve a school's image.

Anthropologist John Ogbu believes the source of poor school performance to be cultural. Schools are failing because they are running into a cultural wall. The white majority assumes that blacks want to incorporate white culture. Ogbu has suggested that blacks resist this cultural imperialism because it is not very useful in the inner city. Inner-city survival skills are more important than school skills. These inner-city strategies rely on the collectivization of economic resources and employment in the underground economy. Their attitude toward school is characterized by distrust and suppressed resentment. Ogbu observed:

> Blacks reject segregated schools because they are judged inferior and distrust desegregated schools because they suspect that these schools perpetuate inferior education through many subtler devices such as biased testing, misclassification, tracking, biased textbooks, biased and inadequate counseling, and so on. Furthermore, Blacks doubt that the public schools understand their children's education needs. There is a strong feeling that the public schools do not understand the Black male student, in particular. Thus, Blacks tend to attribute the low school performance of Black males to schools' inability to relate to Black males in a way that will help them learn.[31]

The suspicion in the black community is that there is a conspiracy to cripple black males who are about to compete with their white counterparts. More importantly for this study, teachers, both white and black, are considered agents of miseducation. Ogbu concludes that cultural inversion is used to offset the anti-black cultural messages. Accordingly, says Ogbu, this resistance to school denies the fact that black children are so busy resisting these messages that they miss the opportunity to learn work discipline. Thurow's observation about education still holds.

> Education also is one way for workers to show that they have "industrial discipline." Having gone through the educational process, the worker has demonstrated an ability to show up on time, take orders, do unpleasant tasks, and observe certain norms of group behavior. These characteristics are also fundamental to the work process. Often they are more important than specific job skills. Many manpower training programs report that industrial discipline is more difficult to teach than specific job skills. Schools may or may not teach these economically desirable characteristics, but traditionally they have provided the employer with an opportunity to find out whether the individual does or does not have them.[32]

Individuals leaving high school with or without a diploma are faced with a relatively hostile labor market. It is impossible for black mayors to lure new industry with a poorly educated workforce. The reputation of poor schools discourages investors and developers, yet school officials continue to engage in the same old self-serving politics. In 1977 Mayor Young admitted as much: "I don't think we can restore this city to real economic health until we restore our schools."[33]

Corporate Responsibility and School Reforms

With the collapse of the manufacturers, economic warnings were sounded. Local schools know there are few local jobs for high school dropouts or graduates. Since the schools cannot stop educating potential workers, there have been several attempts to reorient the learning process. Leaders of the economy and schools do not operate in a vacuum. Occasionally businesspersons offer school officials advice. At first glance, the situation appears to be a classic example of non-communication between two sectors of society which are interdependent. A closer look shows a great deal of "signaling" taking place.

Businesspersons signal school leaders through advertising their employment needs. At one extreme, local businesses hold job fairs for graduating seniors and, at the other extreme, they import workers. In most cases the businesses exercise their civic responsibility by offering to directly assist the school system. The so-called Detroit School Compact in which the school received direct contributions from businesses is an example of this cooperation. Businesspersons commit themselves to hire Compact students and help those who want to go to college. Marion Orr analyzed the development of the Compact and decided that politics of Compact-making must include strong support from the mayors and the community. In an interview with Orr, Mayor Young declared "the compact is a lot of talk and no money."[34] The mayor also believed that the program was "elitist" and that the assistance would never reach the children that needed it the most. Orr concluded,

> The compact alone is not a cure-all for Detroit's social and economic ills. It is important, however, because it illustrates that it is possible to put human capital-

enhancement policies on the local agenda. But while the Detroit Compact has made its way onto the local agenda, it remains to be seen whether it will stay there. Key ingredients—involvement, mobilization, and motivation of the nonbusiness elements of the community—are missing.[35]

Schools play a critical role in the labor market. High school graduates constitute the largest number of workers entering the secondary labor force. Schools and businesses understand this relationship. The problem is that there are simply not enough high-paying jobs to accommodate those workers leaving high school. Within the present job market situation, a high school graduate may have to compete with school dropouts for menial jobs. Accordingly, schools have received the message that the local labor market is flat. Therefore, it is wise not to overpromise students about jobs. Equally disturbing is the prospect that businesspersons, who are expected to signal schools, have no clear idea what the phase "better educated worker" means or how they plan to use such a person.

Summary

The failure of the nation to invest in the human capital of inner-city residents contributed to the inability of Rust-Belt cities to compete in a post-industrialized and international economy. The role of inner-city schools was never defined by American industry. Without signals about how black workers will be utilized in the new economy, inner-city school officials were left to drift. The signals were not given because the leaders of industry are not sure about their need for labor. Schools cannot reform their curriculum until they are in the loop of the employment cycle.

There is a clear need for a statewide, if not a national, job strategy. The resources necessary for a systematic job-matching between available labor and job opportunities haven't been found. Yet little is being done for these potential workers at any level of government. No one seems to know what to do. As Mayor Young said, there is a lot of talk but no money. It will take massive amounts of training to improve the job-readiness of the current generation of inner-city residents, to say nothing of their progeny. George Bush, proclaiming himself the "Education President" and launching a 1989 summit for governors, never addressed the issue of school employment nexus. Until it is addressed, the chances of school reform are limited.

NOTES

1. See Daniel Bell, *The Coming of the Post-Industrial Society* (New York: Basic Books, 1975)

2. Paul Tiffany, *The Decline of American Steel* (New York: Oxford University Press, 1988), p. 186.

3. Interview with anonymous source.

4. Sam Robert, "Newark's Loss May Really Be Its Renaissance," *New York Times* (April 8, 1991), p. 1b.

5. Wilber Allen "Mayor's Policy and Development Office" in *Newark: An Assessment*, Stanley Winter, ed. (Newark: New Jersey Institute of Technology, 1978), p. 48.

6. See Douglas S. Massey and Nancy Denton, "Hypersegregation in U.S. Metropolitan Areas: Black and Hispanic Segregation Along Five Dimensions," *Demography* 26, (1989):373-392.

7. Ibid.

8. William Goldsmith and Edward Blakely, *Separate Societies* (Philadelphia: Temple University Press, 1992), pp. 133-134.

9. See Gary Becker, *Human Capital* (Princeton: Princeton University Press, 1975).

10. Bruce Nussbaum, "Needed: Human Capital," *Business Week* (September 19, 1988), pp. 101-102.

11. Pierre Boudieu, *Outline of a Theory of Practice* (Cambridge: Cambridge University Press, 1977).

12. See Wilbur Rich, *Coleman Young and Detroit Politics* (Detroit: Wayne State University, 1989).

13. Data Resources, Inc. *Metro Insights* (Lexington: Regional Information Group, Data Resources, 1989), p. 316.

14. Ibid., p. 317.

15. Data Resources, Inc., *Metro Insights* (Lexington: Regional Information Group, Data Resource, 1988), p. 318.

16. Ibid., p. 380.

17. Goldsmith and Blakely, op. cit., p. 80.

18. Data Resources, Inc. op. cit., p. 391.

19. Data Resources, Inc. Ibid., p. 683.

20. Ibid.

21. Ibid.

22. Ibid., p. 682.

23. Ibid.

24. Ibid., p. 681.

25. Ibid., p. 684

26. Ibid.

27. See Peter Eisinger, *The Politics of Displacement* (New York: Academic Press, 1980).

28. Jeremy Rifkin, *The End of Work* (New York: G.P. Putnam's Sons, 1995), p. 12.

29. Ibid., p. 77.

30. See Robert Catlin, op. cit.

31. John Ogbu, "Diversity and Equity in Public Education," in *Policies for American's Public Schools: Teachers, Equity and Indicators*, Ron Haskins and Duncan MacRae, eds. (Norwood, NJ: Ablex Publishing Corporation), p. 144.

32. Lester Thurow, *Generating Inequality* (New York: Basic Books, Inc. 1975), p. 88.

33. Jeffrey Hadden, "Young Urge New Method of Public Financing," *Detroit News* (December 28, 1977), p. 1b.

34. Orr, op. cit., p. 119.

35. Ibid.

Conclusions

This book has pursued three related themes. The first was to determine the emerging relationship between black politicians and school policy. The second was to explore the role of schools in an uncertain local economy. The third was to examine why school reform failed after the black takeover. The school politics of Detroit, Gary, and Newark schools is very suggestive of post-industrial urban school politics. The study tried to highlight the similarities as well as the idiosyncratic nature of school politics in each city. I found that the takeover of public schools by black politicians in these three cities had differing impacts on the extant politics. My research suggests that the black political leaders in each city were by-products of the local political culture. This was particularly true of black mayors, as they were unable to penetrate the defenses of the school cartels or to influence city economies. The central staff of the board of education were so bureaucratic and tradition bound, that outsiders did not stand a chance at fashioning remedies for dysfunctional schools. It is difficult if not impossible to graft school reform on this system.

Recall that in Chapter one, I outlined the "stages" of black participation in school politics. School integration, so central to the early stages, is no longer part of the discourse of the current stage. The new school leaders find stewardship saddled with financial uncertainties, underachieving students, and a shrinking job market. Given their penchant for rambunctious board meetings, the new board members are not able to make a case for more investments in their communities. Stories about wayward board members, low SAT scores, fiscal mismanagement, incompetent teachers, inadequate facilities and equipment have fallen on deaf ears. Nothing seems to be able to rally Americans to save inner city schools. Warnings about America falling behind other industrialized nations economically don't seem to move policy makers. What, then, can be done about inner city schools? The answer lies in the relationship of schools to the political economy. Instead of being reactive, schools must be proactive. The current mix of politics and education inhibits rather than enhances the school's ability to be proactive.

The Current Mix of Schools and Politics

Political scientist Harmon Ziegler believes that a number of factors account for the breakdown of the traditional separation of city politics and the internal politics of boards of education.[1] He cites four factors: citizen concerns over the quality of education; increasing interaction between city departments and the board; the interrelationship between school policy and other city policy; and federal court decisions impacting schools. This commingling is more apparent in some cities than in others. In our three cities the mix of politics and political ambition did not serve schools well.

There is too much money and status involved in school politics to maintain an effective dichotomy between school politicians and city politicians. Publicly elected officials have adopted a hands-off posture towards school matters, with the exception of finance. This carefully constructed facade disguises a constant struggle between city hall and what I call the public school cartel (PSC). Behind the scenes, and more recently in front of a school activist audience, politicians in this study debated issues ranging from curriculum reform to the possibility of privatization.

The most surprising aspect of public school politics is that school leaders have become so intimately involved in the inner workings of city politics. Former Detroit Superintendent Arthur Jefferson openly admitted that he knew his way around Detroit politics. Other leaders interviewed left no doubt of their political prowess. Yet the more politicized school leaders become, the less able they are to prevent encroachment by elected officials into their political space. This increasingly symbiotic relationship grew as cities began to lose their manufacturing base, and inner city schools found themselves listed as one of the largest employers in the area. Schools have become so large an employer that mayors are kept informed of board spending policies.

School board members in this study had dual personalities. Their motives fell between the old idea of noblesse oblige and outright machine politics. School politicians subscribed to both these impulses. As the case study shows, board members were "true believers" or shameless stipendiaries. In their view, their actions were in the best interest of the schools as well as in the public interest. This may explain why the mayor's ruminations and complaints about schools fall on deaf ears.

Mayors and School Policy

My study suggests that the mayor is in an awkward position from which to dictate school policy. Mayoral encroachment into school policy arena is replete with perils. If a mayor's policy preferences are congruent with the school activist community, then he or she can promote initiatives without fear of reprisals or embarrassment. If not, the board and its supporters will try to "reeducate" the mayor. If that fails, then the mayor is lured into the political thicket of school politics. Mayors in this study retreated after a series of political punctures. Those mayors who stay in the school policy arena risk alienating one of the most powerful interest groups in city politics, teachers unions.

Mayor Kenneth Gibson of Newark was effectively isolated from school politics when the teachers union mobilized for an elective board. The switch to an elected board further insulated the mayor's office from school policy. Union leaders became his chief critics and worked to defeat his bid for reelection. Throughout Gary Mayor Richard Hatcher's tenure, he attempted to steer the board toward more pedagogic innovations and enjoyed some success during Superintendent McAndrews' term but was less successful thereafter. Detroit's Mayor Coleman Young took a relatively low profile in school matters throughout his twenty years in office. Nevertheless, he was not afraid to publicly endorse incumbents in board elections. He saw these actions as a part of his role as titular head of Detroit's Democratic Party. Occasionally he advocated a larger role for city hall in school policy. When he did, the press listened, but the PSC members politely ignored him.

This reluctance of mayors to get deeply involved in public school matters is not because they are without political resources. As the highest elected official in the city, the mayor is expected to address all the problems of city life. The most important mayoral resource is the media. Local media, particularly newspapers, seem hungry for news about schools. Mayors can use the media to gain leverage but not to control school policy. A mayor's complaints can become city headlines. A sustained hortatory initiative, coupled with widespread public dissatisfaction, can be effective in accelerating change in board composition and superintendents. The mayor, not the superintendent, is the civic teacher of the community. Superintendents, particularly those recruited from the outside, cannot hold the media's attention for very long. Herein lies the power of the mayor in school policy.

The use of the bully pulpit seems to be more effective than allowing the mayor to appoint school board members. When mayors are granted the power to appoint school board members, it is not absolute. Besides upholding a tradition of appointing professionals, the mayor of Gary was also obligated by law to appoint representatives from the opposite party. Most of Hatcher's appointments were considered acceptable to the school cartel. Goldhammer believes this practice is due to an informal screening process that weeds out personalities who would cause problems for the sitting board members.[2] This finding holds for Gary some thirty years later.

Based on this review, we conclude that mayors must meet at least six preconditions if they want to exercise leadership in school policy: 1) control over the appointment process or a strong voice in board candidate selection; 2) credentials as a professional educator (i.e., either having worked as a teacher or having relatives in the teaching profession or equivalent credentials); 3) substantial financial input into the school budget; 4) statutory authority to mediate racial integration disputes and union/board conflicts; 5) media support during school crises; and 6) the political respect of school activists. Without these essential prerequisites, mayors are powerless in school policy.

School Board Elections

In this study school board elections were biased toward incumbents, union-backed candidates, and middle-class professionals. Detroit's school elections have always been competitive and are held in off mayoral election years. Although nonpartisan, school board campaigns are rarely fought over different visions of school policy. Most are purely contests of personalities. The exception was the 1988 HOPE reform campaign in Detroit. The HOPE team lost its momentum shortly after assuming office and most of its members in the subsequent election. In this study a school board position was considered a stepping stone to political insider-ship.

Mayors do endorse school board candidates and contribute to school campaigns, but their influence in elections is far less than that of the teachers unions. As the Detroit schools drifted from one fiscal crisis to the next, Mayor Coleman Young stood foursquare in his support of every millage election while in office. However, Young was not able to dissuade the board from signing collective bargaining agreements for which there was no foreseeable funding source.

Whereas Detroit has always had competitive board elections, Newark board politics are less competitive. In Newark elections are administered by the board staff and are characterized by low turnouts. The composition of the Newark board did not change radically with the transition to any elective system. Charles Bell has remained president of the board throughout the transitions from an appointed to an elected board and from Mayors Ken Gibson to Sharpe James. It is true that elected boards are more representative but do not necessarily lead to outsiders being elected.

Wayward School Boards

In this study the black takeover of school boards signalled no fundamental change in policy. The actual takeover was preceded by an apprenticeship to white cartel supporters. One of the consequences of this socialization or co-optation is that black school board members became comfortable with the old ways of doing things. This gradual socialization explains why the governing norms of the boards is "to get along, go along." The result is that new members adapt to these norms, and the adaptation inhibits any real change in policy. Besides socialization, there is a series of state laws and regulations that prevent any fundamental changes in the way school boards function.

In each of the case studies, the role of the central board staff in governance was not obvious. Central board staff prefer to express their preferences privately to board members. They seldom publicly express their views on policy. When new policy is at variance with old policy, the staff can delay or sabotage efforts at the implementation stage. As most of the literature on small bureaucracies will attest, the behavior of the central staff is not unusual. They protect their administrative prerogatives from itinerant superintendents, conflictual board meetings, and muckraking newspaper reporters.

In our three cities, the queue for school board membership was long. Board membership was a sought after political prize. School board membership can be characterized as part school-booster, superintendent-overseer, and local politician. The rush to serve on the boards of education in the three cities stem from a variety of motivations, not the least of which is membership in the so-called school cartel. For some school board members election also represented a start in local politics. For others it is the culmination of years of community activism, PTA work and booster activities. Despite the fact that school board membership is part-time, extremely low paying, and only episodically newsworthy, school activists spend an incredible amount of time and energy seeking these positions.

Black activists who saw board membership as yet another vehicle for turning the community around were clearly disappointed. However, they discovered that school governance is more complicated than they expected. The biggest surprise for new members is that they were elected purchasing agents. The school is a buyer and the marketplace is replete with salespersons, exhibits, and product developers. Vendors sell everything from buses to metal detectors. Consultants offer services ranging from computer programming to management workshops. The schools, considered good buyers because of the large orders involved and the political nature of decision-making, are targets of high-powered sales pitches from book publishers, curriculum material developers, and computer companies. Board members have been offered all types of discounts, perks, and incentives to purchase a particular brand or product for their schools. Vendors create special marketing items for minority board members and contribute to the members' campaigns for reelection.

Aside from vendors, the member is subjected to a variety of other forces. Former Newark board member Daniel Gibson supported this view. He states that "urban boards of education are conducive to becoming the community employment agency. The primary mission is not to educate the kids but find employment for the community. Their primary concern was to get money and employees."[3] It seems the longer a board member serves, the more cynical he or she becomes about school reform. Board members lose faith in the public relations schemes which show progress toward school improvements. Throughout their tenure they are subjected to endless new teaching methods, school management ideas, teacher initiatives, and federal mandates. Vendors, administrators, and consultants invent endless new approaches to inner-city students' learning problems. The Second Gary Plan is an example of an administrator-generated innovative program. Detroit's School-Based Management initiative and all-male academies are also examples. None of these reforms lived up to their promises.

The motives for board membership have changed. The new people believe that they serve as a matter of right rather than obligation. Some members succumb to nepotism, favoritism, and conflicts of interest. Board members become wayward when faced with these new and tempting opportunities and then they become frustrated at the inertia of the school bureaucracy. As a consequence, in-fighting and petty politics consume a disproportional amount of the member's time. This makes dissatisfied board members easy targets for muckraking reporters.

Reporters are always looking for good stories. Newspaper, radio, and television reporters deliberately seek bizarre stories about local school board infighting, ineffective educational practices, and fiscal mismanagement. Embellishments and exaggerations help hold the attention of readers and viewers. City dailies have learned that their suburban readers enjoy stories of scandals, corruption, and misdeeds involving city politicians. The type of coverage can hurt the image of public schools. Although the so-called cartels do not seem to fear the media, such reports can generate a call for action by the state legislature.

What Can the State Do?

The state legislature seems powerless to stop the deterioration of the inner-city schools. We have suggested earlier that the relationship between state and local districts is extremely complex. There is no doubt that the state has the legal authority to take over schools for any reason it deems appropriate. This was done in Newark. It is too soon to predict the impact of this takeover but the resiliency of the Newark school cartel will be tested. The state of New Jersey takeovers of the Jersey City and Paterson school districts have drawn mixed reviews.[4] It is difficult to reverse the effects of practices that produce under-performing students. Consequently, states prefer interventions during financial emergencies. This may be good policy in the suburbs, but it has hurt inner city schools. State responsibility should not end with mere provisions of mandates and money for inner city schools. Money and mandates are not enough. Schools in this study need more supervision and oversight. States cannot accept the assurances of the local school cartels that they can do a better job with more money. The way inner-city children are taught must be changed.

The crisis in schools is not over who controls the schools but rather what level of government is responsible. Without the ability to fix responsibilities, it is difficult to make school reform work. The choice that states face is simple: either gain more control over local school boards or risk writing off most of the children in those schools.

Is this a case for more state control? The local district system, as it is now constituted, promotes racial and class apartheid. As our case studies demonstrated, local entrenched interests were pursued at the expense of children. More state regulations and inspections could potentially protect the learning opportunities of poor children.

In interviews for this study, administrators and local school leaders were adamant about maintaining local control. They saw it as part of an American tradition and yet another access point for minorities in the decision-making process. They were committed to fight any expansion of state control. Since education is the largest item in the state budget, local officials fear an expanded role for departments which could easily create an even larger bureaucracy. A more powerful state bureaucracy would inhibit local initiative and innovation, so the argument goes. Meanwhile, local districts in this study are mired at the bottom of the state hierarchy in terms of school performance.

The alternative to state takeover is a federalization of public schools. This alternative was not supported by any of the participants in this study. No educational interest groups have gone on record in support of this idea. However, America cannot continue to operate effectively in a postindustrial world without some consistency in the quality in its public schools. A black student in Gary has the same right to a first-rate education as his/her white counterpart in the suburbs. One cannot, however, make the argument that federalization produces more bureaucracy. As this study suggests, inner city schools are infested with bureaucrats. The task now is to create some standardization of the school curriculum and teacher quality. You can't get there without more federal initiatives. Otherwise, we will allow schools in Germany and Japan to remain the best in the world economy, and American school graduates will continue as second- and third-rate applicants in the post industrial labor market.

Schooling for a Post-Industrial America

Sociologist Daniel Bell suggested that a new national economy based on advanced technology, knowledge, and information is replacing the current manufacturing economy.[5] Heavy labor-intensive manufacturing, at least as we knew it, will no longer dominate the world economy. Many blue-collar manufacturing jobs have been exported to so-called Third World nations. American industry and its counterparts in the European Common Market have become the world's financial, communication, and high-technology centers. American leadership of the international economy, if there is to be any, will revolve around financial and research resources. It follows that a more educated work force is needed.

This reshaped economy is a global one with interdependent labor and consumer markets. A college education will be the minimum requirement for entry into the best jobs in the labor market. The dual labor market predicted by economists has become a reality. The primary labor markets will include those jobs with security, high salary, and status. The secondary labor market will consist of low-skilled and temporary work. The composition of the new work force will not only change school curriculums but also the politics of cities. H.V. Savitch predicts:

> The rise of post-industrialism changed urban politics, both in America and abroad. Political brokerage and monumentalism could no longer suffice. Energetic and imaginative policy leadership was required. The new politics faced the task of collecting bits and pieces of the social structure in order to build a vastly more complex city. To do this, policy direction would have to replace laissez faire, and collaboration would be a better substitute for unbridled competition. Post-

> industrialism also required immense investment from
> the private sector, whose risks would be mitigated by
> state guarantees.[6]

Currently, there is little enthusiasm among investors for this type of investment venture. There appears to be little, if any, signs of such a realization on the part of politicians in this study. They seem to be just coping, not planning for the future. If industrial capitalism required only a few black workers, then postindustrial capitalism could need even fewer. Uniformed workers such as security workers, public safety workers, and food service workers will represent the best jobs in the black community.

The old corporations will give way to newer firms. Finance, real estate, research and development corporations, communications, etc., will stand at the apex of the economic pyramid. The new primary labor market will be dominated by educated workers with post-secondary educations. Black workers will not be competitive because of their lack of education. People will be judged by the amount and quality of their schooling. Although school officials are aware of these scenarios, they are not in a position to make any changes. There is a tremendous amount of cynicism and resignation about improving schools in the inner city.

The Futility of School Reform?

Books and articles on school reform flow with regularity, but few success stories are recorded and fewer innovations are institutionalized. Americans have been told often that schools are headed to hell in a hand basket, but, unfortunately they believe the crisis is confined to inner city schools. The general public seems interested only in controversial curriculum policies such as sex or religious education. In order for any reform policy to work, it must have the enthusiastic support of all Americans.

If inner-city schools are so bad, then we should get children out of them. If the classroom teaching can only accomplish so much for these children, then organize the learning process differently. It is not that educational policymakers are unaware of what is wrong but rather that school politics are so nebulous that solid and rational reform cannot be built on the present organizational foundation.

This mushy foundation has become a quicksand for blacks who now lead inner-city schools. They have inherited a system that is old, bureaucratic, and financially unsound. Unlike their white predecessors, they have less political space between them and regular politics. Ineffective governance has become the norm. Black school children are still behind their white counterparts. Violence in schools continues unabated. The cost of maintaining schools continues to escalate. The results of these elements have been excruciatingly painful for the black school leaders. The reason that the agony has continued for so long is there is no way to deny blacks their chance at governing schools. Poor school performance and mismanagement are not enough. Having a board with a black majority is not enough. Recruiting black superintendents is not enough. An African American curriculum is not enough. As my review of school politics shows, Gary, Detroit, and Newark school boards made decisions that often reflected the interests of school interest groups, not the students. There is no evidence that the poor are better off under black-led school boards. The governing school boards are not free to introduce new curriculum or to change personnel policies. State laws protect the traditions, rules, and norms of the *ancien régime*.

Saving Public Schools

The image of public school educators needs to be improved. The loss of the cultural authority of public school teachers is exemplified by the numerous critical national and local reports of the eighties. These reports charged that the public schools were either mediocre or operating with low standards. They called for widespread reform of the curriculum and teacher evaluation. This assault on the cultural authority of public school educators was made possible because tests showed that American students are far behind students in other industrialized nations.

Accordingly, the public school cartel may be in danger in the long run. As the social norms which protect teachers and administrators from performance scrutiny erode, educators could be faced with rebellion from parents and more supervision from the state and federal government. Reports such as *Nation At Risk* are a tremendous indictment of the present system. The reputation of the public schools is so poor that inner city parents can be mobilized to support a voucher system that allows private entrepreneurs to educate their children. Potentially, this could be a serious challenge for the public school cartel.

The threat from private schools seems far off but the consequences of a shrinking labor market is relevant to society now. Simply put, America is not investing enough human capital in inner-city students. More specifically, the linkage between school curriculum and the post-industrial economy remains tenuous. The nation seems to be gambling that it will not need most black workers. It is a high risk wager. Unfortunately, the research in this book cannot answer the core question concerning inner city school policy: How do young blacks and other minorities fit into the new emerging economy? Since it is impossible to answer this question in a clear and direct manner, school reform is problematic.

The questions raised about reform in this book are not restricted to inner city schools. Recall the *Nation at Risk* report criticized all schools. The supposedly successful suburban schools are not exactly free of the uncertainties of the new economy. The problem of unpreparedness for the new economy is not limited to African Americans. If Jeremy Rifkin and others are correct , then it is just a matter of time before most white-collar jobs are affected. It behooves us to rethink the nation's education policy and reassess the people who govern it.

Leaders in the three cities in this study seem to be aware that political control is not enough, but they are suspicious of any attempt to impose educational reform from the outside. In 1968 Professor Charles Hamilton made a similar observation.

> It is absolutely crucial to understand that society cannot continue to write reports accurately describing the failure of the educational institutions vis-à-vis black

people without ultimately taking into account the
impact those truths will have on black Americans.
There comes a point when it is no longer possible to
recognize institutional failure and then merely propose
more stepped up measures to overcome those
failures—especially when the proposals come from the
same kinds of people who administered for so long
the present unacceptable and dysfunctional policies
and system.[7]

Twenty-six years later, the same people are still writing
education reports, but school politics in cities has drastically
changed. Blacks have achieved political control but not the cultural
authority to make fundamental changes in educational institutions.
Black politicians aspire to this authority, but the uncertainty of
their economic environments and nuances of black politics
preclude any fundamental change in school policy in the
foreseeable future. This should enrage all thoughtful Americans
and make them less comfortable about our economic destiny.

NOTES

1. See Harmon Ziegler and K. Kent Jennings, *Governing American Schools* (North Scituate, MA, Duxbury Press, 1974).

2. Keith Goldhammer, "Community Power Structure and School Board Membership," *The American School Board Journal* 130 (March 1955), pp. 23-25.

3. Interview with Daniel Gibson, April 7, 1995.

4. See Abby Goodnough, "Jersey City and Paterson: Mixed Results for State," *New York Times* (April 14, 1995), p. B6.

5. See Daniel Bell, *The Coming of the Post-Industrial Society* (New York: Basic Books, 1975).

6. H.V. Savitch, *Post-Industrial Cities: Planning in New York, Paris and London* (Princeton, N.J. Princeton University Press), p. 285.

7. Charles V. Hamilton, "Race and Education: A Search for Legitimacy," *Harvard Educational Review* 38, 4. (Fall 1968), p. 671.

INDEX